BIRTH OF THE BAD BOY

John skated backward, dropped his gloves, rolled up his sleeves, then stopped, knees slightly bent, fists bunched, like a boxer. He grabbed the oncoming jersey hard. His left fist came up, level with his eyes, and he threw a punch. . . .

The forward's body slumped, fell inward to his knees, and John straddled him, a handful of jersey and his left fist cocked. His face, hot, full of blood, not bleeding, but burning . . .

Sweat was all over him, in his hair, his eyes, mouth. There was a pounding noise, sticks and skates into the boards by his team bench. His teammates were cheering, rowdy, showing their approval. . . .

And up in the air, the sound of the crowd, roaring their approval too . . .

The feeling of accomplishment was tremendous.

The John Kordic Story

The Fight of His Life

Mark Zwolinski

SEAL BOOKS
McClelland-Bantam, Inc.
Toronto

This edition contains the complete text
of the original hardcover edition.
NOT ONE WORD HAS BEEN OMITTED.

THE JOHN KORDIC STORY

A Seal Book / published by arrangement with Macmillan Canada

PUBLISHING HISTORY

Macmillan Canada edition published 1995
Seal edition / November 1996

CIP: 95-931504-7
All rights reserved.
Copyright © 1995 by Mark Zwolinski.
Cover photo copyright © 1996 by Richard Arless, Jr.
No part of this book may be reproduced or transmitted in any
form or by any means, electronic or mechanical, including
photocopying, recording, or by any information storage and
retrieval system, without permission in writing from the publisher.
For information address:
Macmillan Canada
A Division of Canada Publishing Corporation
Toronto, Canada

ISBN 0-770-42733-2

PRINTED IN CANADA

UNI   0 9 8 7 6 5 4 3 2 1

Contents

Acknowledgments

THERE ARE DEBTS owed, and debts paid, in the making of this book. Debts of gratitude to the coaches and general managers—Jean Perron, Pat Burns, Doug Carpenter, David Poile, Pierre Page, Dave Chambers, David Andrews, Tom Senregret, Ray Lemaire—without whose willingness and patience to talk openly on a very difficult subject, this book would not have been possible.

To John's buddies—Michel, Tim, Raj, Charlie, Mario, Leslie, Phil, Sam, Mike, Magic—and dozens of others who made life easier and more fun for me.

For the pain they went through, in recalling their memories of John for me, there can be no simple way to say thanks: Sandy and Nancy, the best to you always.

To two first-class men: Bob Goodenow and Gary Bettman, for their time during the NHL strike, which was at an absolute premium.

To Paul Bouchard, simply for your time and understanding.

To the wonderful journalists who preserved countless details and memories: Peter Chaney, Rosie DiManno, Scotty Morrison, Bob McKenzie, Frank Orr, Damien Cox, Red Fisher, Russ Doyle, Vak Verakaitis, Kevin Johnson, Mark Spector, Martin Paquet, and Jacques Teasdale.

A special thanks to *Toronto Star* Queen's Park reporter Lisa Wright, whose advice during a very trying period of writing was greatly appreciated and whose level of professionalism I am still trying to live up to.

There were also others who gave their time—lawyers, coroners, drug therapists and counsellors, hotel owners and staff, police officers, and ambulance attendants—men and women who became embroiled in the tragedy and who simply wanted the story to be told truthfully.

There were eight cities visited—Vancouver, Portland, Seattle, Edmonton, Toronto, Montreal, Quebec City and New York—and 187 interviews conducted for this book. Given that many of the interviewees wished to remain anonymous, or were "challenging" to be around, there is a debt of gratitude and a debt paid in their acquaintance. It's never easy to dredge up the past—it simply had to be done.

Given, too, that many of the interviews required a translator, this book simply could not have been written without Louise Lepiné. There was not one single contribution that could have been greater than hers. Louise, I wish I could speak French to say you will always be special to me . . . but there, I said it anyway.

It must be understood, before reading this book, that some of the descriptive detail is based on the recollections of those mentioned above. The remaining descriptions are built from John's recollections; stories he told me during our all-too-brief friendship.

To Nicole, my editor, for whom I would stand in the way of a bullet. I can only wish all writers could be as lucky to work with someone as special as she is. To my line editor, Liba, who endured what I guess was the dark vanity of my pride and still did a wonderful job. And to my publisher, Denise, for believing in this book.

Throughout the year it took—from signing a contract to reading edits—my wife Iris Duncan endured more than was necessary. She was forced to tread where no one else would. If there should be kudos, the credit is hers.

And lastly, to John himself: there is the memory of your own desire to write a book about your experiences. What a book that would have been. I only hope this is what you would have wanted it to be.

Prologue

JOHN KORDIC lost everything he ever was—or was going to be—August 8, 1992. He was 27 years old. He had fought with ten police officers. It was the last fight of his life.

Most people, including the media, his close friends, and fellow hockey players, knew only what they read—that John tangled with police during a rage induced by coke, alcohol, and steroids. To this day, the truth of what the police actually did to John remains obscured.

The Kordic family, still embroiled in a $1.6 million lawsuit against the police, ambulance, and City of Quebec, believe there's more to his death.

The truth is, no one was really surprised by John's death: rumors of addictions and debauchery plagued his seven-year NHL career. It was a popular belief—and one based on his failures through what appeared to be countless second chances, given to him by his NHL employers—that John was on a course to self-destruction. Now, more than three years after his death, to believe that premise is to believe a lie.

On the night he died, John was disconnected from every support system he had: his fiancée, his family, and—perhaps most significantly—hockey.

According to a toxicology report, he was lethally high on cocaine—120 milligrams per 100 milliliters of blood—

and would have likely died even had he not met with police intervention. John, however, routinely consumed equal, and even greater quantities of the drug. Cocaine was his support system, tragically so, and was allowed to develop out of the ignorance and inability of those who claimed to have given him the umpteen second chances to remain in hockey.

To this day, the number of officers alone is enough to raise questions.

John's mouth opened as he took his last breaths. The police around him cared only to keep him subdued. They failed to recognize the tell-tale sign of the onset of a cardiac arrest: a bubbly white froth, mixed with blood, which dribbles out of one's mouth. John lay there, pathetically, no longer a hockey player, a son, a brother, or anything—rendered pathetic.

In the final analysis of the inquest into his death, John died a cocaine addict who abused alcohol and ravaged his health through an advanced steroid program.

The inquest itself—a 39-day probe spread over a seven-month period between October 1992 and April 1993—became the definitive statement of John's final days. Though there were suspicions raised in the press about the conduct of the police, coroner Gerald Locas, who presided over the inquest, exonerated police and the attending ambulance technicians. Locas, in fact, shocked most observers by making a single recommendation—that ambulance technicians, in the future, be educated to recognize the effects of cocaine on patients, "for the better protection of life." After 39 days, this solitary, toothless recommendation seemed absurd and suspect, even to the casual observer.

The police escaped reproach. Locas, who admitted among friends that the number of police alone in John's room raised his own suspicions about their conduct, emerged from the inquest thoroughly convinced the two police forces were merely adhering to their respective codes of conduct in taking John down.

There were, however, several key points which were never fully explored.

Paul Bouchard, the Kordic family lawyer, was denied

by Locas when he requested an examination of a taped conversation over the police radio at the time John died. Bouchard, who had hired an expert, was seeking to expose what he believed to be a cover-up. Locas, after consulting with his advisors and police lawyers, decided against Bouchard's request.

John's life, and death, created a huge amount of sensational media coverage. Much of it, though, never delved into the life John really lived, and how he lived it. People were always curious about who he was, and what happened to him—players who knew him, like Cam Neely, Marty McSorley, Mike Lalor, even Wayne Gretzky, as well as hockey fans, intrigued by his tragedy.

John's story is that of a Canadian kid from an Edmonton neighborhood, a former altar boy, who grew up loving hockey, not unlike hundreds of other Canadian youngsters.

His story is a tragedy of sports, and one not soon forgotten.

PART ONE

The Father, the son, and the . . .

Chapter One

ON SATURDAY afternoons, John Kordic served as an altar boy at St. Andrew's Catholic Church in Edmonton, Alberta. John loved being inside the building, loved the silence that permeated every corner, the shafts of light that speared down from the stained-glass windows, and, most of all, the sense of drama. But it was the aroma, common to many churches, a resinous smell strengthened by years of candle burning and incense, that most intrigued John.

John, who was usually accompanied on these afternoons by his best friend, Tim Walsh, had attached a significance to his service as an altar boy: as much as he had to playing road hockey in his 112th Avenue neighborhood until well past the time the streetlights came on.

On those afternoons, John passed through the sacraments under Father John Cunningham's guidance. He knew that without them, a Christian could never pass into the kingdom of Heaven after death. So it was that soon after John's birth on March 25, 1965, in Edmonton, that Father Cunningham made the sign of the cross on his forehead in St. Andrew's baptismal. Shortly after he began playing hockey at age eight, John received his first holy communion, accepting the eucharist from Cunningham's hand. Father Cunningham was, in a sense, John's first coach.

• • •

Ivan Kordic was a master cabinetmaker, and his son's hero.

John's principal aim was to make his father proud. This was his aim as a boy, and became his overriding goal as a young man. There were some who may have even seen it as an obsession. In the three years John had been playing hockey, Ivan was rarely absent from the collection of parents, girlfriends, buddies, and rinkrats who regularly constituted the turnout. Through the worst Edmonton winters, early morning or late evening, Ivan unfailingly lent his support. John was very much aware of the sacrifices his father—his whole family—made so that he could play hockey.

Ivan and Regina Kordic had emigrated from Croatia to Canada in 1963. Both came from tiny villages south of Mostar. Their education had a strong religious base, and they tried to imbue in their children a strict adherence to the teachings of the Bible. They understood work, and they understood hardships, having endured the Second World War.

John, his older sister, Toni, his brother, Dan, and younger sister, Lillian, were taught traditional values in an atmosphere of love, warmth, and support.

John could hear plates being set upon the table as he returned home from church. He could smell his favorite foods, pork chops, onions, potatoes. On the table, there would be a plate of thickly sliced homemade bread.

On nights when it was raining in Edmonton, clear broadcasts of "Hockey Night in Canada" were a treat.

John was in his room after supper, waiting for the in-focus sound of the television set as if it held the suspense of a magician's trick. He looked over at a small pile of schoolbooks. John was in grade seven, at St. Mark's junior high school, and for the first time in his life, he had a significant amount of homework to do. Math was no longer a simple process of long division and learning multiplication tables; now he was confronted with having to learn equations and other logistical principles. He rarely neglected to do his homework.

Underneath the math books were novels and grammar texts. Soon, he would be expected to read works by Margaret Atwood and Margaret Laurence, and to write essays about what he'd read.

For the moment, though, he thumbed through the pages indifferently. His keenest interest was in art. He had discovered that he liked drawing, and that he was good at it. He was beginning to work with paints and bristol board canvasses instead of crayons and limp brown newsprint. He visualized landscapes, desert floors, cactuses, the lazy meander of a fence up a mountain meadow. He would look for meaning in his work, try to see beneath the surface. At times he would try to explain these emotions to Walsh and his other friends, whose reactions ranged from sarcastic giggles to whispers that John was a "deep thinker."

The television set made a static, almost fuzzy sound, like electronic fog. Underneath it somewhere was the voice of Foster Hewitt rising over the introductory notes of the "Hockey Night in Canada" theme.

As for millions of other Canadian households, "Hockey Night in Canada" drew families together in front of the television set on Saturday nights. For the Kordic family, it was a tradition: Foster Hewitt, followed by Wayne and Shuster.

On those nights, John would sit pondering the player who would be wearing number 4. He was quick to remind everyone that his favorite player, Bobby Orr, wore that number. He wore that number, and so did his brother, Dan.

John would chirp about how great Sittler was. Palmateer was also spectacular, and Dave Williams, the Tiger, the Leafs' charismatic penalty king, stoked his enthusiasm. The Leafs were his favorite team, and if Orr was his favorite player, then Sittler, Palmateer, and Williams rated honorable mentions.

Ivan would smile at his son's enthusiasm. He had encouraged John to focus on his education. But he understood his son's love of hockey. Ivan, however, could not accept the fighting. He knew that hockey officials publicly criticized on-ice fighting. Then he saw enforcer-type players batter each other every Saturday night, and wondered at the credibility of those same officials. Although he felt that soccer was a more appropriate game for John, he supported his son's desire to play hockey.

The year John was 12 years old, Halloween had fallen on a Saturday night, and John had refused to go trick-or-treating in favor of watching the game.

There was no denying that John's destiny was pinned to hockey. Everything pointed to it.

Chapter Two

WAYNE MEYER and Percy Kozak live 700 miles apart, but rely on each other to make a single judgment on a hockey prospect.

Meyer, director of player personnel for the Portland Winterhawks, operates out of Memorial Coliseum, a modern, multipurpose facility in Portland, Oregon. There he administers a list of 50 players for each Western Hockey League (WHL) season.

Over the years, Meyer and Kozak, who lives in Edmonton, racked up considerable long-distance phone bills talking to each other about one prospect or another. One such phone call took place between the two men a few days before Christmas 1981.

"Wayne, it's Percy, listen, you've got to come up here and see this 16-year-old kid. I think he's somebody we should be interested in."

"Is he on our list?" Meyer asked.

"Nah, nobody's got him yet. It's crazy, he's the best midget defenseman in the city."

Meyer was skeptical. "What's the kid's name?"

"John Kordic."

Meyer could not recall having come across the name. Virtually every director of player personnel in the WHL was cognizant of up-and-coming 16-year-olds, from Manitoba to British Columbia. They worked with team scouts, as well as with bird dogs (scouts) who monitored rinks in out-of-the-way places. The WHL's scouting reports, updated three times a year, rated each prospect for the league's annual entry draft. Players as young as nine years old were scouted through bird dogs, and future hockey stars were cultivated at ages 13 and 14. It was likely Meyer may never have seen John Kordic play because he limited his scouting itinerary to AA-level games, and when John was a bantam, he played with the Knights of Colombus (KC) A-level bantams.

"Percy, is this kid that good? We've seen them all. Am I gonna be able to tell Portland to list this kid? Is he gonna play for Portland next year?"

"I think you should get up here and look at him, Wayne. He can shoot. He's five foot eleven and 180 pounds . . . he's a big kid, he plays tough, but he's better with the puck. You should see him with the puck."

Kozak went on to praise the Knights of Colombus's big defenseman for his passing—hard, direct, accurate—and his skating, tireless, always picking up his assignment in his own zone.

Later that night, Meyer phoned his parents in Edmonton to tell them he was coming home for Christmas.

For the first time in his life, John's reputation had preceded him. He was among the best midgets in the city, recognized wherever he played. He was almost always seen in his KC's jacket, snug-fitting jeans, and under his jacket a tight T-shirt, even in winter. In the Westmount Mall arcades, where he hung out with his friends, the jacket would come off. There were girls there to impress, pretty ones from Bishop MacDonald's High School, where he was in grade 12.

Cocky and confident, the junior ladies' man strutted his stuff. Over the summer, he had traveled to British Columbia with the provincial under-18 soccer team to compete in the national championships. He was an outstanding goalie, with catlike agility, penetrating vision for the opposite team's attack, and a general dislike for strikers. He constantly challenged the opposition's top shooters, diving fearlessly, recklessly, extending his body fully to snare a shot, and landing hard on the turf, only to spring instantly to his feet, and trash-talk the frustrated shooters. At the time, the Edmonton Drillers, which played in the pro-rank Canadian Soccer League, actively recruited Kordic, much to Ivan Kordic's pleasure. When John returned from the soccer championships, his hair was lightened to an almost blond hue. He described for the curious Walsh how he'd squirted lemon juice onto his head, then gone out in the brilliant West Coast sunshine. Voilà! The desired effect. The lightened locks worked charmingly with the girls at the mall.

When John's stock rose in local hockey circles, Ivan began to behave like an embattled impresario. For example, Ivan was often seen storming from the arena, when John or another player made mistakes or were overly physical. Although Ivan succeeded in establishing his son's position on the teams, usually to John's greatest advantage, he spoke for his son, so much so that, at times, Ray Lemaire and Tom Senregret—John's bantam and first-year midget coaches respectively—were left pondering the young hockey player's naïveté.

Ivan still wanted John to pursue soccer, to become a university athlete like his wunderkind daughter, Toni, a basketball star. He grappled with hockey's apparent duality, with how it could be driven by such athletic grace and beauty, and yet permit, even encourage, violence. In spite of this, however, Ivan did everything he could to advance his son's career. On Saturdays, he frequently drove John to United Cycle on White Avenue. The store's basement, where team sales for local organizations were conducted, became a haven for local teenage sports stars. Ken Hitchcock—"Hitch"—a respected coach with the Sherwood Park midgets, got his start in team sales at United Cycle. Hitchcock often listened to John proudly talk about hockey, his sister Toni's basketball exploits, Ivan's mastery with wood, or his mother's cooking. Sitting in the skate section, John enjoyed fraternizing with other A and AA players, while other youths and their parents milled about, trying to read the crests on the young stars' jackets. Hockey was the basis of John's confidence, the hallmark of his identity, and certainly his raison d'être.

John's team, the Knights of Colombus, were blessed with excellent coaches at every level of their organization. John looked up to Charlie Lemaire's father, Ray, who coached him in bantam, and to Tom Senregret, whose sons Casey and André also played with John in midget.

Senregret introduced his team to a 2–1–2 forechecking system, one of the least complicated and most foolproof styles of attacking the opposition's offense. It relied on two agile, hell-bent forwards to penetrate the opposition zone and pester any puck carrier, while a third forward floated higher, near the blue line or closer to center with the two defensemen. Should a turnover occur in neutral ice, the forwards would be churning up speed in anticipation of a quick pass from the defenseman. It was a strategy designed to produce what had become a buzzword in hockey vernacular: the transition game.

Senregret had a valuable asset in captain Billy Mc-Gregor, whose father, Bruce, became executive vice-president of the Edmonton Oilers in 1990. However, on more occasions than he cares to remember, Senregret had to deal with rebelliousness from McGregor and other key players, who often defied the coach's systems. Senregret was not an overly belligerent coach, which made it difficult for him to manage his way out of these situations. He would have loved a team of John Kordics, players who were quiet in the dressing room, who skated their hearts out when he blew the practice whistle, and who were non-confrontational. Senregret had grown close to John; he respected the young player not only for the strong, clean games he played, but also for his quiet demeanor and irreproachable manners.

The city league was dotted with future NHL stars—Wayne and Dave Babych played for the Maple Leaf Athletic Club, as did Keith Brown and Tim Tookey. Mark Messier played a single season for the KCs. At the time, Doug Messier, Mark's father, ran a hockey school, and between games, and sometimes periods, Senregret marveled at how Doug would bring out a set of boxing gloves for impromptu bouts with his son. Mark never lost.

When Wayne Meyer arrived at the Coronation Arena, John was having the best season of his young career and

Tom Senregret had handed over his coaching duties to Bob Torrey, a personable 24-year-old who had just earned a degree in education from the University of Alberta.

"Where the hell has everyone been?" Meyer asked Kozak as he watched John play. "I can't believe no one else beat us to this kid."

That night, Meyer, not in the habit of staying the entire three periods when scouting an unknown, hung over the railings until the final whistle. After the game, he hopped down the arena stairs and hurried to the dressing-room area. He waited until Torrey had cleared his post-game duties, then cornered the coach in a quiet end of the corridor and introduced himself.

The next day, Meyer dialed the Winterhawks number in Portland. When he finally got through to owner and general manager Brian Shaw, he praised the KC's big defenseman who wore number 4. Enthusiastically, he told Shaw to put John on the Winterhawks' player list. Training camp in Red Deer, Alberta, was still nine months away, but he wanted John's name among the 50 players being invited to camp.

Later that night, he dialed John's number.

"Hello, John, my name is Wayne Meyer. I'm director of player personnel for the Portland Winterhawks. I was at your game last night and we listed you today to be part of our training-camp roster . . . I want you to come and play hockey for us next winter."

John was elated. He had always believed that one day he would play in the NHL. Now, John faithfully devoted every hour to hockey.

John felt positive about everything Meyer said. The franchise, the first junior hockey team outside Canada, the collaboration of general manager Brian Shaw and coach Ken Hodge, the 15,000-seat facility, the likelihood of the Winterhawks being given the nod to host the 1983 Memorial Cup . . . John listened to all of it with unrestrained enthusiasm.

Meyer was an expert warrior in mitigating options outside junior hockey. A popular option was to accept a spot with a junior franchise's tier-two affiliate, and retain eligibility for a lucrative scholarship with a college in the

United States. It afforded the player experience at the junior level, and up to $60,000 in a Division One scholarship. Existing education bursaries in junior paled by comparison.

The chief advantage in signing a major junior contract, though, was its fast track to the NHL. In that path, John saw his dreams realized. Never once did he speak of options.

"We have an excellent team in Portland, and you'll play for that team," Meyer told him. "If you want to be a pro, this is the way you have to go. You'll make our hockey team, John . . . and if you play in Portland, you will play in the NHL."

Over the rest of the season, Meyer tailored his sales pitch in hours of phone calls and visits to the Kordic household. John had asked him to speak with his parents, who were confused and skeptical about the junior system. Meyer explained to the Kordics that the Winterhawks' hands-on approach ensured that each player completed his education. Shaw had successfully arranged several education options for the players in the seven years the team had been in Portland. Players entering grade 12 were enrolled at Reynolds High School, in the upscale neighborhood of Beaverton. The school was located within easily commutable distances of most of the team's billets. Players like John, who needed to complete only a few credits for their high-school diploma, could do so in a correspondence course, under the guidance of a tutor. He told the Kordics that while the team's travel itinerary was one of the league's worst, with some bus rides as long as 16 hours, the coaching staff designated study periods during those trips in which all other distractions—card games, Walkmans, or portable stereos—were shelved in favor of schoolbooks.

Players signed an education contract as part of the standard player contract. John was to be paid $300 a month. His room, board, medical needs, and schooling would all be funded by the team. It was mandatory for a player to appear at schools and hospitals if requested to do so. The team, however, absorbed all expenses incurred by this, not the player. In keeping with the education contract, players were paid between $1,500 and $2,500 at the conclusion of every year they played. The money was kept in trust, and could be retrieved if the player pursued a university education at the end of his junior career. If the player turned pro, the funds became null and void.

In July 1982, John flew to Portland for a two-week stay with Meyer. He met Shaw, Hodge, the rest of the team staff, and was familiarized with the arena, the billets, and the city. He met team star Grant Sasser, who was a local high-school graduate, and even took in a rodeo. Before the end of his stay, he agreed to the terms of the contract, and was ready to sign. First, however, he needed Ivan and Regina to sign a parents' consent form. Meyer returned to Edmonton with John to obtain their signatures. After several evenings of hospitality and negotiations at the Kordic residence, Meyer left town, the requirements of the contract completed.

John had never been happier. He received a crisp new Hawks' team jacket, which mirrored the Chicago Blackhawks colors. Courted by reporters and photographed for the local newspapers, John basked in congratulations and adulation. It was a proud and defining moment for the entire Kordic family.

Ivan Kordic was also given a team jacket, which he wore with pride. John's father was still critical of some aspects of the game, but was resigned to the fact that John was not going to sign up for courses at the University of Alberta. But if his son was going to pursue hockey to its highest level, Ivan was determined to provide him with every advantage. He had come to a decision: he would enroll John in a hockey school.

Chapter Three

AT 7:00 A.M. on a weekend morning in August 1982, Ivan and John Kordic packed the family's Ford Torino with hockey equipment and set out for the Tomahawk Hockey School. The sun was rising out of the east, glaring yellow-white, and the highway was almost free of traffic as they headed to the Enoch Centre Arena. They traveled about 10 miles, then turned left onto a concession road to Enoch. About two minutes down the concession, a sign welcomed them to the Enoch Indian reserve.

Cree Indians own the 2,000-acre-plus parcel of land, most of it lowland fit for golf courses and corn farming. Passing through one of several paved roads that link it with the city, visitors notice the driving mechanisms of dozens of oil wells, the thick bulkheads bobbing languidly. The wells provide a source of wealth for the reserve's inhabitants. The arena, golf course, schools, and community centers are all modern, and several chiefs live in stately homes backing onto the Saskatchewan River, the reserve's northern boundary.

The arena is a huge building of concrete block and sky-blue aluminum siding. Its size made it an obvious landmark to the Edmonton hockey community. Inside the double doors is a large foyer flanked by offices and trophy cabinets. As in countless Canadian arenas, there is a small ticket office enclosed by wire-meshed windows. Just beyond it is a small table with a cash box, a clipboard, and a sign that reads: TOMAHAWK HOCKEY SCHOOL, and below it, SIGN UP HERE

Sitting behind the table, Sue Laforge speaks with other fathers, while behind her, little boys with broken hockey sticks slap around a piece of balled tape. She is helping her brother, Bill, a hockey coach and operator of the hockey school.

Ivan had checked out the school earlier, visiting several times to watch the level of play and quality of instruction. On one occasion, he saw several fights break out. Once the greetings were exchanged, Ivan asked Sue if the school condoned violent behavior.

"Well, I know the coach's philosophy is that nobody fights, because it says so right here in the application form," she told him. "You would be expelled right away for fighting, even on dry land [as opposed to on the ice], your money would be revoked."

She handed Ivan an application form and went to get the coach.

Bill Laforge, a longtime coach at all age levels, briefed John's father on the school's curriculum, assuring him that fighting was not tolerated. Then, Laforge walked Ivan through the facility, walked and listened. Ivan spoke of the University of Alberta and his commitment to education, and of the legendary Claire Drake, the most successful coach in Canadian university sports. He also spoke of Randy Gregg, the Edmonton Oiler great who rose through the city's hockey ranks, then played for Drake before graduating to the NHL. He told Laforge his daughter, Toni, was an excellent student at the university who would likely be a member of the Canadian women's basketball team at the Los Angeles Olympics. Why all the conversation? Ivan had a particular route he intended John to follow; he wanted to make sure Laforge understood what it was.

Back in the lobby, John was happy, enthusiastic. He had just been enrolled in the Tomahawk Hockey School, with his father's blessing. It was a two-week stint that, to him, was like an unofficial announcement that he had arrived in the world of professional hockey.

Chapter Four

RED DEER, Alberta, August 1982, population just over 46,400, sits on the Red Deer River, about 150 kilometers south of Edmonton.

The highway from Edmonton to Red Deer is an asphalt strip through fertile farmland that in the 1960s was coveted by Alberta oil barons who came to fatten their purses on the substantial oil and natural gas resources in the area.

John had completed his two-week course at the Tomahawk Hockey School. He'd skated with Rob Brown, Greg Hawgood, and several other Western Hockey League stars, and had acquitted himself nicely. Now he was on his way to the Winterhawks' training camp in Red Deer. He was nervous, but psyched-up.

After saying goodbye to his parents, he picked up his hockey bag and headed into the Red Deer Arena. John Kordic was on his own.

The hallway inside the building was startlingly empty when he entered. It was the August off-season. The lights were out and no staff seemed to be around. Down the corridor, though, were familiar sounds and smells. Fifty players, filing in for training camp, were talking and laughing, as were trainers, scouts, coaches, front-office staff, and members of the media.

"John . . . John Kordic, how are ya, kid?" asked Winterhawks' general manager Brian Shaw.

John smiled and greeted Shaw. When Shaw turned to another conversation, John began making his way to the nearest dressing room. The one he found was crowded, noisy, full of half-naked players, and equipment. He knew enough rookie etiquette not to ask anyone to make room for him. Several forays later he found a place in a dressing room near the end of the corridor.

The room was relatively quiet, full of young players who didn't know one another, putting on their equipment, and checking straps and laces for tightness. John sat down at an empty stall, next to a tall, lanky player, a rookie like him. The young man introduced himself as Cam Neely. He was 17 years old, the same age as John, and hailed from Comox, British Columbia. They shook hands firmly, and John knew he had found a friend.

"I heard this is a pretty tough league, there's a lot of fighting," John said to Neely later as they skated around slowly, dragging their skate blades behind them in a groin stretch.

"You scrap much?" Neely asked.

John hesitated, searching for the answer. The truth was, he'd played physical for the KCs, but under his father's watchful eye, he'd never gone further than a shoving match in the corner, maybe a glove-hand punch to the head. He'd avoided fighting for two other reasons as well: he could be ejected from a game, and all players wore full-face, metal cages with their helmets.

"Not really," John finally told Neely. "Do you know what goes on here?" he asked.

Each question was met with a half answer, or a new question. Neither had proof, or more significantly, experience. They continued their lazy circling of the ice, reaching out for reassurance that they wouldn't get their heads knocked off.

"Hey, guys, what's the problem?" asked Kelly Hubbard, a bruising, third-year defenseman and veteran of many Western Hockey League fights. He had obviously overheard them.

"We were wondering if there are a lot of on-ice fights," John said.

"You're gonna go someone sooner or later," Hubbard said.

Hubbard listened intently to both players' concerns and was supportive, empathetic, like a big brother.

"Look, guys, look, come here," Hubbard said, using one hand to grab John at the top of his shoulder, near his neck, and placing the other just below John's opposite shoulder. "Now, try and throw a punch . . . You can't because I've got you tied up, you're fucked. Now all I have to do is start throwing and you're buried . . . The last thing you want is for a guy to get a hold of your sweater like this. He can do what he wants and you're basically gonna be eating his fists."

"Okay, you're the brain surgeon, what do we do now?" John said dryly.

"First thing you do is watch the other guys do it, watch and learn from it. The most important thing is to know what the other guy does, what hand he throws with . . . What hand do you throw with?" Hubbard asked.

For a moment, John was taken aback. He'd never given the subject much thought. Suddenly, he did something so swiftly, so assuredly, it felt natural, as if he'd been doing it his whole life. John reached for Hubbard with both hands, the fingers on his right hand clutching the scruff of the player's neck, while his left hand balled into a fist that pumped in pistonlike speed.

"I grab you, then I drill your fucking head before you have a chance to think," John said.

Hubbard smiled. John was a lefty. "That'll screw with a few guys' heads."

"Why's that?" John asked.

" 'Cause just about everyone throws with their right. So most guys look for that, they line up looking for it, they know they have to tie up your right arm so they can throw."

They had broken apart, and, circling, John tried the same move, his left arm cocked beside his eye. He could look right down his arm when it flew at his opponent.

"What are ya gonna do when I do this?" Hubbard said. In one swift motion, Hubbard leaned into John, so tight that Kordic's left was useless. He took John firmly by the chest, jerking him so that he stumbled forward, the blade on his right foot coming down hard and chipping the ice.

Before John knew what happened, Hubbard thrust him back upright, totally off balance, and had his sweater tied up. Kordic was perfectly ripe for a beating.

"How'd you do that?" John asked.

"Just watch," Hubbard said, smiling slyly. "It's time to separate the men from the boys."

Hubbard continued his little initiation course with the two rookies, drawing some stares and smirks from other players. At over six feet and 190 pounds each, Kordic and Neely didn't need much tutoring. They had seen the craft plied enough times to realize that this wasn't some public-school game. They were rock hard and young. And they were quick learners.

They were skating again, this time with dozens of other players. "Who the fuck was that guy?" John asked Neely as Hubbard skated off. "He's crazy."

John fell readily into the drills and scrimmages. He was open to advice and worked hard with bulldog determination and endurance. He put his head down and skated until he was told to stop. He never complained.

Wayne Meyer ran training camp while Winterhawks' coach Ken Hodge and general manager Brian Shaw looked on from the bench or the stands. John noticed several other men, in suits or hockey jackets, who were always looking. They were part of the emerging landscape of pro hockey, faces and voices, even smells, that brought a peculiar feeling of fear to the young rookie. He worked harder when they were around but he couldn't suppress his nervousness.

Meyer was in his junior-hockey swan song conducting the Hawks camp. Over the summer, he'd accepted an offer from the Detroit Red Wings and would soon be Western Hockey League scout for the NHL team. Meyer had seen a lot in his 12 years with the Hawks. In the previous season, he'd enjoyed a tremendous sense of accomplishment over the franchise's first ever presence at the Memorial Cup. These sentiments carried over into training camp, despite a fourth-place finish among the four best junior teams in Canada. Now Shaw had pulled off a major coup in boardroom politicking to bring the week-long championship to Portland, and Meyer wouldn't be along for the ride.

His final year of service was excellent in terms of recruiting. His script for the annual WHL entry draft was unfolding according to plan, with the Hawks signing Ray Ferraro and Randy Heath. He'd also hustled the team's resources to sign John Kordic, in his opinion the luckiest find of all.

Chapter Five

EVEN WHEN it is filled to one-third capacity, Memorial Coliseum in Portland, Oregon, is still formidably noisy. These hockey fans usually gravitate to the first two seating tiers around the ice. Among them are gangly boys, some wearing oversize Hawks jerseys, who scramble after stray pucks and shout at players to flip a few extras over the glass during warm-ups. Teenage girls hover around the seats adjacent to the walkways from the dressing rooms or mill about near the rear exit after games. They have their favorite players, the best-looking of the bunch, and the sweet anticipation that among the rookie recruits there may be one or two cute ones.

The Hawks' activities are covered in the local daily newspaper, *The Oregonian,* or on radio through Dean Vrooman. The Hawks also have a fan club, which publishes a newsletter, and a radio show called "Hawk Talk." Unofficially, membership includes socializing with the players beyond the regular fans' access.

The Portland Winterhawks opened their 1982–83 season in September with about 6,500 fans in the stands. As had become customary with home openers, Shaw and Hodge were introduced over the public-address system, along with the players. The Hawks were the defending WHL champions, and had finished in first place in three of the last four seasons. It was also customary to applaud wildly when the conquering heroes returned for their first game of the new season. The fans didn't disappoint.

John was introduced. His skates, stick, jersey, helmet, and full-length hockey pants were all brand-new. The lights were down, and a spotlight followed him as he covered the short distance from the bench to the blue line where the rest of the introduced players, in their Winterhawks home whites, were lining up. The applause was loud, the cheers, ear-splitting. He was psyched, ready to play for the largest crowd he'd ever played for.

Brian Shaw also absorbed the adulation, finding it exquisite.

He'd brought hockey to Portland six years earlier, a pixilated move in the eyes of many of his WHL colleagues, but one that they now respected. His attendance figures vaulted to the top rankings among all major junior teams in Canada. In November 1982, two months after the marvelously well-received home opener, he was banking on approval from the WHL to host the Memorial Cup, Canada's national championship at the major junior level. It would mark the first time the event would be held outside Canada, and would underscore Shaw's arrival as the most influential owner in major junior hockey.

It was clear that Shaw liked to embellish that image. For example, he drove a Mercedes-Benz and liked to park it in front of the Coliseum, next to spots allotted to top brass from the Coliseum's number-one tenant, the Portland Trail Blazers of the National Basketball Association. His suits were expensive, tasteful, and always pressed. When he drew his cigar to his mouth, there was flashy jewelry on his fingers and a chic watch around his wrist. Hawks fans recognized him by his plume of cigar smoke and tanned skin, which, with his slightly balding, golden-brown hair, thick eyebrows, and full, confident laugh, gave the impression of an acquired man.

Shaw was also one of junior hockey's great survivors. He had been fired from the St. Catharines, Ontario, junior A team in 1970, and in 1974 from the Edmonton Oilers, which were then a member of the World Hockey Association. Determined to operate his own franchise, he formed a group that included Vancouver Canucks defenseman

Howard Snepts, and bought the floundering Edmonton Oil Kings in 1975. After a money-losing year in Edmonton, he brought the team west to Portland and won the respect of local fans and his peers across Canada with a third-place finish. He also retained Ken Hodge to take the coaching reins of his franchise. He had been a coach, with the Moose Jaw Canucks of the old and forlorn Western Canada Hockey League, a team that had had Dave "Tiger" Williams as a stick boy and Hodge as a promising defenseman until an errant stick in the eye ended the latter's playing career—and launched his coaching career—at age 21. By the 1980–81 season, Hodge had the Hawks rocketing to a 56–15–1 record, and a second-place finish behind a remarkable Victoria Cougars team.

Success on the ice means success at the box office, and that's where Shaw went to tap into the power and influence he craved. Four years earlier, the Hawks drew 2,800 people on a Wednesday night. By the 1980s, a crowd comprising fewer than 4,000 fans was a disappointment. Shaw used this increase in attendance in his strategy to sway the WHL to approve Portland as the next Memorial Cup host. But many members of the WHL board of governors were skeptical about his ability to guarantee sponsorship money. Moreover, they were concerned about the event's reception in an American market still learning about the sport. Molson Breweries and CCM, the hockey-equipment manufacturer—the Memorial Cup's primary sponsors— were waffling on their commitments. League president Ed Chynoweth was an ally of Shaw's throughout the negotiations, but could only offer marginal assurances about sponsorship when pressed by the media. "At this point," he said to *The Oregonian* reporter, "CCM is unsure it wants to continue its sponsorship and Molson will not be involved as in the past because the brewery is not represented in the western United States. Television coverage of the final game is planned, whether by Canadian or U.S. networks, and Molson has indicated that it will remain a sponsor of the broadcast."

Another stumbling block arose in the form of the Ontario Hockey League's (OHL) stalemate with the Ontario Hockey Association (OHA) over revenue sharing. The OHA suspended the OHL based on the latter's refusal to hand over part of its profits. Since the OHA is a member of the Canadian Amateur Hockey Association (CAHA), the CAHA also suspended the OHL, pending resolution of the matter. This left a cloud over the Memorial Cup because the CAHA administers the event, and the OHL's participation must be inclusive for the event to truly represent a national championship. Chynoweth showed Shaw's boardroom clout when he said in *The Oregonian,* "We, the WHL, have signed an agreement with the OHL and the Quebec Hockey League that the three leagues will play for the championship this spring . . . If Ontario [Ontario Hockey League] gets back with good graces, it will be no stumbling block at all. I'm not trying to kick aside the idea of playing for the Memorial Cup, we would be more than happy . . . I'm just trying to say that we will play for a championship cup. It could be called the ABC Cup or the Brian Shaw Cup. Brian is one of the few guys around who can afford to buy the cup."

Shaw, standing near center ice on a red carpet rolled out for the pregame ceremony, waved to the adoring fans. He turned to acknowledge all corners of the arena. John and several other players smirked as a host of politicians huddled beside Shaw and took their bows. John peered across the ice, at the other blue line, where the opposing team, the Seattle Breakers, were lined up. The players looked huge, menacing, and for a moment, his heart sank. He removed his helmet for the national anthem, then a quick whistle from the referee and a command from one of his own players: "Let's go, boys."

He would remember this Saturday afternoon in September as his first game as a professional hockey player, but for the moment, there was barely time to take it all in.

The game was typically fast. John got hit, and he laid out hits. He made mistakes, but he held his own.

In the second period, the puck shot past the Hawks' bench, and John rammed a large forward into the boards, stopping him from chasing it into the Hawks' zone. The two players shoved, to break free, and his opponent's elbow came up into John's mouth. The forward attempted to get back into play, but John's stick found the man's midriff, hooking him hard, grinding him to a halt. A hand now, on John's stick, ripped it away angrily. The forward, whipping his gloves to the ice, came at John bare-fisted.

John skated backward, dropped his gloves, rolled up his sleeves, then stopped, knees slightly bent, fists bunched, like a boxer. He grabbed the oncoming jersey hard. His left fist came up, level with his eyes, and he threw a punch. He could feel a burning pain on the side of his head, his ear, and his cheek. He was being repeatedly punched in the face.

Anger now, not fear. Fuck fear. The left struck true. The forward's body slumped, fell inward to his knees, and John straddled him, a handful of jersey and a left fist cocked. His face, hot, full of blood, not bleeding, but burning. Then arms in front of his eyes, around his chest, pulling him. A linesman breaking it up. It was over.

Sweat was all over him, in his hair, his eyes, mouth. There was a pounding noise, sticks and skates into the boards by his team bench. His teammates were cheering, rowdy, showing their approval. "All right, Kords . . . kicked his fuckin' ass, Johnny K."

And up in the air, the sound of the crowd, roaring their approval too. Even as he skated towards the penalty box, fans pounded on the glass, exuberant, and from everywhere, it seemed, came clapping and a wall of sound. The feeling of accomplishment was tremendous. The fans seemed to share in it, revel in it. Up to that moment, their attention had been held by high-octane offense and winning teams. Fighting was handled, when it was called for, by veteran Brian Curran, with Hubbard in a supporting role. But Curran was injured, and unofficially a void existed. The team had seen dynamite, a diamond in a haystack. They'd never witnessed one of their own dismantle a player the way Kordic had. They'd never seen a player who could throw a left like that.

In the penalty box, John wiped his face with a towel. His lip was swollen. It stung when the towel passed over it.

His jaw was numb, and his teeth hurt. He looked over at the forward drying his hair in the opposite box. The player's head was covered by the towel. John wasn't even sure who the man was. He hadn't seen a name or number, and he couldn't see one now.

The announcer identified him: Jamie Cayford, a call-up trying to add some toughness to the Seattle lineup.

Not anymore. The door to the box opened again. John was ushered out, this time to the dressing room downstairs. His penalty was five minutes for fighting, and a ten-minute misconduct. Fifteen minutes. There wasn't fifteen minutes left in the period. He was effectively being neutralized from the game.

In the dressing room, he flung his helmet to the ground, letting it crash into the wall and spin on the floor. Ice. He wanted ice, and a trainer brought him some. His face hurt, everywhere. He sat down, grimaced, and hung his head. He was exhausted, but he could get back at it. He knew that much.

Suddenly, the dressing room door burst open. It was Hodge and Shaw, coming at him.

John's heart sank. But Hodge was animated, smiling. So was Shaw. Hodge congratulated him and said he never knew John could fight that way. He was impressed. Shaw echoed the coach.

After the game now, out into the lobby. A rush of fans, dozens of them, with praise and autograph books. Many had his team picture, which they'd purchased from the souvenir stands only minutes earlier, and which they wanted him to sign. All of them wanted to be next to him, to say hello, to welcome him. Then a woman who said she was with the Hawks fan club wanted to arrange a time when he could be interviewed for "Hawk Talk." And there were girls with pretty faces working their way through the throng, then stopping beside him, and smiling.

He had sparked it all. It was exhilarating. A boost to his ego. But it was so new, it was all so brand-new.

Chapter Six

IN THE BEDROOM of a Wood Village home, 20 minutes from Memorial Coliseum, John looks into a mirror.

His face is swollen and hurts too much to touch.

"C'mon, ya big pup, are we going?" Mike Ellingboe, 14, says.

"Yeah, hang on a minute."

One last look in the mirror, then John hurries down the carpeted stairs to the hallway and the front door. On the way out, he pokes his head into the kitchen.

"Hey, Mom, are you gonna use that?" John says to Kay Ellingboe, who is peeling back a plastic bag from a loaf of bread. "I need it for my sandwiches."

"The whole loaf, John?"

"Yeah, sure, it's going to be a long road trip."

Mrs. Ellingboe shakes her head lovingly and smiles.

The Ellingboes are John's first billets, and the only player hosts who live in the Wood Village area. The rest of the billets are located near the arena, or in Beaverton, a suburb on the other side of town. Every year, the Hawks designate families to provide room and board for the team's players, for which they are paid. They are signed to contracts by Shaw, and every spring, after the close of the hockey season, they gather for a barbecue where Shaw tells the host families if their contracts will be renewed. The agreement specifies that each player's room be equipped with a private phone line accessible only by the coach and the player. The phones help management enforce the team's curfew. Calls are made randomly, and Hodge fully expects the player to answer. Shaw isn't above making agreements with the billets to report any breaches of conduct. Many hosts are willing collaborators since their winters revolve around the players and they don't want to be released as billets. Some billets, like the Ellingboes, have had relationships with players cut short by Shaw because he considered them too lenient.

It had been almost two months since John had arrived in Portland from Red Deer. His friendships had grown, with Neely, Hubbard, and many of the other players. His hockey career, and his life, seemed to have been on fast forward. At first, he'd been intimidated by the level of skill of other players. There were centermen, quick on their feet, hooking and slashing at his legs. In the corners, he was often slammed into the boards. When he shoved back, it was against wingers who equaled him physically. He remembered Hubbard's quip at the training camp about separating the men from the boys. At times, he found himself doubting his own talents, then quickly he would clear his mind, and get on with playing the game. John had already earned a reputation as an enforcer.

Hodge had earmarked him as a tough, aggressive defenseman who could take care of forwards along the boards and in front of the net. Hodge knew his players: he had an eye for their strengths and weaknesses. He was also one of the first coaches in junior hockey to adopt the bold practice of leaving only one defenseman on the blue line during a power play. His playbook contained three player patterns for man-advantage situations—1–2–2, 2–2–1, or 1–3–1—with the numbers read from the goalie out. John needed to absorb this and transform it instantly on the ice. He was pegged as the fifth or sixth defenseman on a talent-rich blue line, but circumstances thrust him into a more prominent role. Veteran Brian Curran suffered a broken ankle in the Boston Bruins training camp, and was lost to the game for three months. Another veteran, Jim Playfair, remained with the Edmonton Oilers for the first month of the season before he was returned to junior, and teamed with John.

Although Hodge praised John for his big slap shot and

his ability to ignite the transition game, the coach often singled him out in practices for extra skating. The players hung their heads when Hodge ordered the penancelike drills, and dubbed them "Wallys."

The Hawks practiced at Skateworld, which wasn't far from the health club in Beaverton where the team had carte blanche membership. As a facility, Skateworld was more suited to figure skating because of the short boards around the ice. When Hodge ordered up a session of Wallys, players skated hard across the width of the ice, stopping at the boards and jumping over them, then jumping back onto the ice, bolting to the other side, and repeating the jumps. John was full of rookie mistakes, especially in practice drills, and he often paid the penance in Wallys, along with Hubbard, his first defense partner. Hodge would yell, "Kordic, start skating . . . Hubbard, join him." Hubbard only made matters worse by asking, "How long?"

"Forever," Hodge barked.

The penance was grueling. John told *The Oregonian* he felt Hodge was picking on him. He never understood that Hodge's motives were entirely professional. The coach's mandate was to raise John's skating skills to a higher level. Hodge firmly believed John was going to play in the NHL one day, and like other good junior coaches, it was his job to mold a player accordingly. If that meant skating Wallys, then so be it.

John had spoken to his parents several times over the past two months. The last thing his mother said to him when he phoned from Red Deer was, "Please, Johnny, no fighting." On one of their visits, they saw John in an uneventful bout, but were displeased, especially Regina. "You are not here to fight, Johnny," she told him sternly. John stressed that he had to protect himself, to which Regina replied, "We didn't send you here to protect yourself like that. What kind of example are you setting for your sisters, for Danny." Surprisingly, given his opposition to on-ice violence, Ivan sided with his son.

By the time Ivan and Regina came to Portland, John's reputation in the WHL was as one of the most feared fighters, his rookie status notwithstanding. What stoked all the hype, and instilled fear in many players, was John's ability to take a punch, and his apparent ambidexterity: he had a blinding left hand, but he could throw with the right, with both hands, in effect. He was completely reckless, throwing from everywhere, and at the same time fighting with the style and grace of a boxer on blades. He was, irrefutably, the league's most classic fighter.

John proudly delivered complimentary tickets to his parents at their hotel before heading to the Coliseum. Earlier that day, they had visited the Ellingboes, who marveled at some of Ivan's tales from his homeland, and at his ability to communicate in five languages.

When John arrived at the arena, he noticed the Seattle Breakers had a new face in their lineup, and he immediately understood why. The Breakers had felt John's fury on opening day, had heard all the talk about John's skills as an enforcer, and had played him since. They were afraid of him. They'd summoned Scott Walker from Tier 2 to match up against him.

When the inevitable clash erupted, John grappled with Walker, took a couple of punches, then landed heavily. Walker lost his balance, was at John's waist, and taking more punches. His mouth was bleeding. On the way to the penalty box, he called John a dirty son-of-a-bitch. There is an understanding among enforcers that when one scores a decisive victory over the other, no extra punches are thrown. Such an act amounts to an insult, and too many insults means an enforcer may soon be out of a job. Though they may verbally abuse each other, there is supposedly a mutual respect for their roles. John had not yet adopted that respect, and Walker wanted another piece of him in the worst way.

While sitting in the penalty box through their respective five minute penalties, they spewed profanities at each other, agreeing they would go at it again the second they stepped back on the ice.

The second go-around was no contest. John smashed Walker into submission. The fans knew it, too, knew the subtext to the battle, and rained down chants of *Kordic! Kordic! Kordic!* Victorious, he stood over Walker, pumping a fist into the air.

Ivan and Regina did not share in the adulation. They promptly picked up their coats and left the building.

John was interviewed on "Hawk Talk" after the game.

"John, you've showed everyone how good a fighter you are in your rookie season, but the thing everyone wants to know is where did you learn to fight like that?"

"From my mother," he said. He was standing outside the dressing room, a microphone held near his mouth. There was laughter from the interviewer and from a crowd of fans nearby.

"Well, that's not something you hear every day, but John, you stand over your opponents, and you jab your fist in the air. It's awesome."

"Yup, my mom did that to me, the standing part, any-ways."

Mike Ellingboe was standing at the doorway to the exit corridor.

"Where are my parents?" he asked the boy, walking up after signing autographs.

"Uh, they split, they went back to the hotel."

Later, when John knocked on his parents' door at the Red Lion Inn, his heart was pounding. He knew he was in trouble.

Ivan answered, but held the door ajar. He spoke only briefly, tersely, then slammed the door shut.

A blankness, an emptiness, as John's mind raced. He felt hot. He fumbled as once more he rapped against the door, lightly this time. No response from the other side. Then his open palm slapped the wall.

The drive home seemed to take forever. When he finally reached the Ellingboes and let himself in, Richard told him that Ivan was on the phone.

"I don't want to talk to him," he told Mr. Ellingboe.

Richard asked Ivan to call back, then tried to reason with John. John listened for several long minutes. Finally, he drew in a deep breath and agreed with Richard; he would call his parents back.

This time, they listened, and they understood.

The last words John said were thank you. He said them to Richard, then went upstairs to bed.

Chapter Seven

ON NOVEMBER 17, 1982, Brian Shaw and WHL president Ed Chynoweth called a press conference in Portland to announce that the Memorial Cup would be played at Memorial Coliseum the following May.

The announcement was a triumph for the city, and the biggest feather in Shaw's cap. Shaw was going to walk away with a boatload of money in spite of the apparent lack of enthusiasm from the junior championship's two major sponsors, CCM and Molson Breweries. The Hawks controlled virtually all of the spinoff business—concessions, team-ware sales, and so on—and took a percentage of the gate, which was arranged with the city in the team's lease of the Coliseum.

As far back as the 1980 season, Shaw dropped hints to the press that he was masterminding the transfer of one of several troubled NHL franchises to Portland. The disclosure, though tenuous, panned out into favorable stories in the local media. When real opportunities arose, with the Colorado Rockies, the Washington Capitals, and the Pittsburgh Penguins all looking for buyers, he was never considered a serious player. During the Memorial Cup season, Ralston Purina put the St. Louis Blues up for sale, but Shaw wriggled off the hook, explaining the acquisition of a professional franchise would spell economic suicide. He was right; Memorial Coliseum seated fewer than 15,000 people. The lack of capacity alone was enough to quash any legitimate chance Portland might have had as an NHL

city. Moreover, fans, accustomed to paying $4.50 to
watch a Hawks game, would have to accept as much as a
400 percent hike in ticket prices for the privilege of being
present at an NHL game. Portland fans may have swallowed
such a dramatic price hike for the spectacle of pro hockey,
but the seating problem made the entire gesture irrelevant,
and Shaw's overtures pure rhetoric.

But there were more pressing problems as the Memorial
Cup drew nearer. The Hawks, along with the Broncos,
rose to become the league's most fearsome juggernaut,
which parlayed wonderfully into added Memorial Cup
hype for the hometown fans. Cam Neely was easily the
league's top candidate for rookie-of-the-year honors, firing
56 goals and 64 assists. He blossomed into one of the
WHL's top wingers, a legitimate first-round NHL draft
choice, who periodically stood up for John against opposition enforcers. Neely also became a triggerman on the
power play, along with Ken Yaremchuk, Randy Heath, an
82-goal scorer, and Brian Curran and Jim Playfair on the
points. Yaremchuk returned to Portland three weeks into
the season after hanging on with Chicago in the NHL.

Portland, appearing hugely dominant for the play-offs,
finished the regular season on top of the Western Division.
During a first-round play-off match with Regina, though,
Regina Pats' coach Bill Laforge accused Hawks' management of feeding their players performance-enhancing
drugs. Laforge did not have proof, but felt that it was
impossible for a lethargic Hawks team to suddenly over-
come a three-goal third-period deficit to wipe out his team
for a three-goal margin of victory. He argued that in the
second period, the Portland players received an "upper" of
some kind—an amphetamine, a steroid, or cocaine.

Laforge lodged his protest with Commissioner Chynoweth immediately after the game and demanded a for-
feit. His accusations were heard, but never acted upon.
Without hard evidence, there was nothing Chynoweth
could do. Not about to back down, Laforge held a press
conference. The details may have made good copy, but he
lacked credibility. The man had his enemies. In 1981, he
struck a coach and player beneath the stands in Oshawa,
Ontario, when he coached the Ontario Hockey League's

Generals. A year later, on April 30, 1982, he was accused of sparking a bench-clearing brawl after the Hawks beat his Pats 5–3. The incident was widely referred to as one of the ugliest in WHL history, and Chynoweth suspended three Regina players and ordered Laforge to post a $10,000 bond for the next game. His brazen comments and philosophy about aggressiveness and fighting, his fiery manner with players, and draconian tactics—like keeping players' meal money or fining them for lackluster performance—did not earn him points in the WHL. He was labeled a loose cannon by some of his peers, who may have indulged in similar practices but would never admit to them. Many players, though, loved Laforge, and it was through them that the level of his commitment became public. Many of them sat at his dinner table regularly, his door was always open when they needed shelter, and he operated a special, private phone line which players could use in times of personal trouble or duress. The player simply dialed "F-O-R-E-V-E-R," and was told by Laforge he could do so for as long and as far as his professional career took him.

Ultimately, Laforge was ordered by Chynoweth to retract his comments in a letter of apology to the Winterhawks.

Shaw flatly dismissed Laforge and his accusations when called upon for comment. He also had the support of the WHL brass, which similarly dismissed Laforge's claims.

Rumors, however, persisted, filtering down to the press, with reporters trading off-record tales about the proliferation of performance-enhancing drugs in the Hawks' dressing room. The buzzword was "turbos," a substance reportedly wrapped in aluminum foil and distributed to certain players to take during the game. The dressing room itself was referred to as a "candy factory."

This kind of talk was rarely brought up in Shaw's presence, and when it was, it enraged him. He countered such accusations by enlisting sports psychologists, local police, and the WHL's own security staff. Prior to the Hawks' first Memorial Cup appearance, though, team star Gary Nylund initiated a public-relations disaster by bringing several damning allegations against Shaw, Hodge, and the

entire Hawks' organization. Nylund, who went on to become a first-round pick in the 1982 NHL draft, told reporters that he was being forced to fight instead of play
hockey. He also alluded to the team's rampant steroid use.
The story was picked up across Canada, and prompted
Shaw to threaten Nylund with lawsuits. Eventually, however, the story lost its clout, and the controversy died.

The following year, Shaw introduced junior hockey's
first drug program. Through John's years with the Hawks,
no positive test results were ever reported in the media.
John, though, often talked to the Ellingboes' son, Mike,
about alcohol and marijuana abuse by some of his teammates. He told Mike he was one of about five players who
weren't abusing any substance. According to Kordic, most
of the players drank heavily at parties, while five of them,
including two team stars, smoked dope regularly. John
also said that one player took LSD regularly. Much of this
activity went on at private team parties, during which
players felt they could break most of Shaw's team rules.
The parties also gave the players a chance to meet girls,
with Shaw and Hodge none the wiser. Shaw consistently
discouraged players from having steady girlfriends, reasoning that the players were too young to get involved.

Between the politicking, his daily administration of the
team, and his efforts to keep his players in line, Shaw
worked long, hard hours. Unfortunately, when the Memorial Cup finally rolled around, he didn't have time to enjoy
the fruits of his labor.

Less than a month before the championship, a series of
bizarre events and bad luck befell Shaw's goaltenders. Ian
Wood, who started the opening-round series against Seattle, sustained a cervical spinal injury early in the second
period of a 5–2 win. The Hawks went on to sweep the
Breakers 4–0 in games, but Wood was lost for the remainder of the season. That left the Hawks with Bruno
Campazzi and alternate backup Ed Jones, but Jones had
stretched ligaments in his thumb on April 13 and had a
cast on his hand. Shaw feverishly worked the phones, going so far as to acquire the help of the RCMP in tracking
down Greg Holloway, a seldom-used alternate with the
Kelowna Wings, up in Fort St. James, British Columbia.

The Hawks went on to oust Victoria to win the West Division title, setting up a WHL championship meeting with the East Division champion Lethbridge Broncos. The WHL title tilt was anticlimactic for the Hawks since they were already guaranteed a berth in the Memorial Cup as hosts. The Broncos, who needed the league title to advance, played inspired hockey and took advantage of the league rule book against any procedural infractions by the Hawks. An 8–5 Hawks win, which knotted the series at 1–1, was played under protest when the Hawks started Holloway. The Broncos contended Holloway was eligible only if Campazzi was injured. Shaw countered by saying Campazzi's hamstring had been injured twice in the regular season and was not 100 percent healthy. The Hawks also skated affiliate player Ray Pavlowski in warm-ups, which drew another protest from the Broncos because it put the Portland roster one over the league-ruled limit of 21. "I miscounted," Shaw told reporters sheepishly.

The Broncos, led by brothers Rich and Ron Sutter, went on to clinch the series 4–1 in games to post their first-ever WHL championship since the franchise joined the league in the 1974–75 season. Ron Sutter fired two goals, giving him 22, two short of a league play-off record. He also recorded an assist for 40 points in 18 play-off games to lead the WHL.

On May 3, 1983, five days before the championship was to open, Shaw was back in the boardroom and on the phones, defending his acquisition of goalie Mike Vernon. He entered a tug-of-war with the Lethbridge Broncos, which was also hotly pursuing Vernon as an ace for the upcoming championship. Vernon, the league's Most Valuable Player (MVP) the past two seasons, was the top goalie with a .326 average, and three shutouts in 50 games played. A Calgary Flames draft pick, he had also appeared in two NHL games in Detroit and Montreal, and anchored the Canadian team at the world junior championships in the former Soviet Union. He also played for Portland in the 1981–82 Memorial Cup in Hull, Quebec. After several hours of threats and heated negotiations, Shaw finally won the right to the hockey star's services.

Meanwhile, John fell into a late-season slump, and

while the Hawks were rising to glory, his role as a defenseman, and as the team's top enforcer, diminished. He was taken off the power play. Bolder now, more resolved to stand up for himself, he had several meetings with Hodge to protest. His complaints, however, failed to change anything. At the same time, John acknowledged that his overall effectiveness had slipped a notch or two.

With the play-offs fast approaching, John got into a fight with Alan Kerr during a game with the Brandon Wheat Kings. John quickly thrashed Kerr, prompting the officials to step between the two combatants once it was clear who the victor was. John later confided in Mike Ellingboe, as he so often did during his rookie season, that the scrap was the answer to his slump. It troubled Mike that instead of a big goal or a key assist, John's performance intensified after a good fight.

The Hawks opened the Memorial Cup on May 8, 1983, with a 7–6 win over the Verdun juniors, which boasted 103-goal scorer Pat Lafontaine, the top scorer in major junior. The following afternoon, the Hawks leveled tournament favorite Oshawa Generals 10–5.

Ivan and Regina Kordic came for the championships to watch John play. It concerned them that John seemed to be sitting on the bench more often than he was playing. Before the last round-robin game, John's parents complained to Hodge about their son's absence from the power play. The Memorial Cup, they knew, was junior hockey's grandest showcase, widely attended by pro scouts and general managers; a lack of exposure for the 17-year-old at such a crucial time could prove detrimental when he reached his NHL draft-eligible age at 18. Hodge, who normally tried to avoid such confrontations, was caught off guard. He was considered an excellent bench coach; his teams were always prepared mentally and physically. His coaching style, however, was to always remain objective, to never elevate one personality over another. There was never any question that Hodge thought highly of John. But Ivan and Regina—and John—were not bigger than the team.

The Hawks lost 9–3 to Lethbridge in their final round-robin game, but advanced to the finals based on their two wins, while Lethbridge bowed out with a 1–2 record.

The social highlight of the week-long event was the memorable awards banquet, an elegant affair for everyone associated with the championships. The most prestigious honor went to Pat Lafontaine, who was named the Canadian major junior player of the year. He had 137 assists to go along with his 103 goals, the best single-season scoring feat in junior-hockey history to date. Other nominees were OHL representative Doug Gilmour of the Cornwall Royals, and Dean Evason of the Kamloops Junior Oilers, representing the WHL.

On Sunday, May 14, 1983, the Hawks clinched the Memorial Cup title with an 8–3 win over the Oshawa Generals in the championship game before 9,547 fans.

Shaw could finally bask in a measure of glory. The happy throngs in the stands chanted, "USA, USA, USA," recalling the miracle on ice at the 1980 Olympics. Later, after the diplomats scooped a portion of the spotlight, after the champagne was uncorked, the players had a party of their own. They converged on Hubbard's backyard, which had an in-ground pool. Shaw, ever-diligent, asked the local police to station a cruiser near the premises to ensure no player would drink and drive. He had also guaranteed a team trip to Florida if the players delivered a championship.

A week later, the team was in Fort Lauderdale. The first day, John, disregarding advice, covered his lily-white skin in baby oil, burned to a crisp, and had to spend the rest of the trip indoors.

Chapter Eight

ON JUNE 8, 1984, John was back in his Edmonton bed-room. In a few hours, he would find out whether or not he was a high-round choice in the NHL entry draft.

He was 18, a full season removed from the Memorial Cup championship. He recalled that during his rookie year, a Chicago Blackhawks scout said on a radio talk show that the only players he was impressed with were Grant Sasser and John Kordic. Coach Hodge, not big on handing out the compliments, told him he was almost as-sured of going late in the first round.

Over the course of his second season, numerous scouts made overtures, and he made himself as visible as possible. He knew he'd attracted interest from the New York Rang-ers and the Montreal Canadiens. Wayne Meyer was now chief scout in charge of Western Canada for the Detroit Red Wings, and had spoken to him numerous times. There was also a remote and spine-tingling possibility that the hometown Edmonton Oilers would select him.

John had read the newspapers, surveyed stories on the top prospects, the rankings scooped from the NHL's central scouting bureau, and the accompanying bevy of charts and prognostications.

He had saved a clipping from the *Edmonton Journal,* which pegged him as a shoo-in to be drafted in the first three rounds.

John listened to coverage of the NHL entry draft over the radio, live from Montreal. Between the idle chatter of the broadcast hosts, he could hear the Forum, alive with the hum of several thousand people gathered for the annual rite.

There was an equally high level of anticipation in John's household. Regina was preparing a celebration around a huge dinner. Ivan, in anticipation of a first-round selection, had promised to take the family and John's friends to the chic restaurant Château Lacombe.

When the magic moment came, the announcement of the overall number-one pick, Brian Lawton acknowledged the cheers of the crowd and strode to the podium to pull on a Minnesota North Stars sweater. Lawton was followed by Sylvain Turgeon (Hartford Whalers), Pat Lafontaine (New York Islanders), and Steve Yzerman (Detroit Red Wings). Then it was over, the first round had come and gone, and with it, the live broadcast.

Once more John reflected on his last season and decided he had left an unflattering impression with scouts.

Moreover, at the end of the season, Meyer had reported that John had become a risky draft selection because the young player was prone to moodiness. Meyer would never sabotage John's reputation. He wanted John to succeed, and he admired Ivan and Regina. At the end of the 1983–84 WHL season, however, he acknowledged that John had gone from a promising, accessible player to one whose relationship with his coach had deteriorated, and whose performance had suffered accordingly.

After opening the '83–'84 season at 0–2, the Hawks won ten consecutive games. The tenth win came in early November, and by the middle of the month, *The Oregonian* mentioned John as a possible selection to the world junior championships in Sweden in December.

On November 19, Shaw traded defenseman Jim Playfair to Kelowna for hard-rock defenseman Craig Butz, who they'd lost to the Wings in the '82 expansion draft. To that point, Playfair had been paired with John and together they were arguably the best defensive pair in the league. Playfair's trade distressed John. He placed much of the blame on Shaw and Hodge. Playfair, though, was also in his final year of junior eligibility. A week after the trade, Edmonton recalled him to the NHL. He never played a game for Kelowna and was traded by the Wings to Calgary. Shaw's pipeline to the NHL was obviously well connected; he came out smelling like a rose.

John was glad when Cam Neely was returned to junior by the Vancouver Canucks on October 22. Neely's stay, however, was short-lived, and underscored the way some NHL teams did their bookkeeping.

Neely's return appeared to coincide with the Canucks' purchase of a Boeing 727 aircraft, which was acquired to ease the team's overwhelming travel expenses from the West Coast. According to the *Vancouver Sun,* the airplane cost in excess of $3 million. Neely, meanwhile, was approaching a game limit after which a number of monetary bonuses in his contract were supposed to kick in. He was flourishing under general manager Harry Neale and coach Roger Nielson. He was playing regularly on a line with Thomas Gradin and Darcy Rota, and had scored his first NHL goal against the Toronto Maple Leafs in September 1983. At the time, an agreement between the NHL and junior hockey stated that if an underage draft pick played more than ten games in the NHL his first season, the NHL club was required to compensate the player's junior club with a $15,000 stipend. Shaw added to the controversy, claiming clauses in Neely's contract could boost the total to $50,000. With the Boeing on the team's ledger books, Neely played seven games for Vancouver, then was sent back to Portland. He was recalled December 8, around the time John learned he would not be attending the national junior team camp. Randy Heath, an 82-goal scorer in the Memorial Cup year, was the lone Hawk selection.

The 10–2 record was a distant memory by the new year, and the Hawks went on to finish the year at 33–39.

John was no longer billeted with the Ellingboes. Shaw introduced him to Chuck and Barb Olson, who lived with their charming, close-knit family in Beaverton. He was to be billeted with them. Upset by the news, John asked Richard Ellingboe why the Ellingboes didn't want him back. Richard took the line of least resistance, saying that the family had no say in the matter. Later, John gave the Ellingboes a picture of himself in uniform, with the inscrip-

tion: To the family I love and most wanted to be with . . .
No. 4, John Kordic.

Craig Butz and John Kordic were on a collision course.
Hodge had arranged a drill during practice in which John
was to stand in front of the net, as a forward, attempting
to deflect a shot from the point. Butz was charged with
clearing out the goaltender's crease.

Physically John's equal at six foot one, 190 pounds,
Butz quickly got his stick high, near John's face, ramming
hard cross-checks to get the job done. John shot back
fiercely, then Butz's stick crashed across Kordic's face,
drawing blood from his nose. They dropped their gloves
and fought viciously. Hodge watched for a moment, then
stepped in with defenseman Tim Lorentz to break it up.
He was pleased with the level of aggressiveness his protégés showed.

John went on to play his worst hockey as the season
unfolded. He was called upon to anchor the defense. Instead, he resorted to rushing the puck out of his zone, the
way he had done, with some success, as a midget. His
giveaways in the play-offs netted the worst results—goals,
two of which led directly to losses. He had one shining
moment, in the sixth game of a seven-game series against
the New Westminster Bruins. He didn't fight, but blocked
shots with reckless abandon, made big hits, cleared his
zone, and directed the puck mistake-free. Afterward, on
the bus ride home, Hodge praised John, exclaiming that
John had almost single-handedly won the game. The consensus among the media and the Hawks front office was
that the game was the finest they had ever seen John play.

The Hawks advanced past New Westminster, needing
three overtime games, before bowing out in four straight
to the Kamloops Blazers, the WHL's top-rated team with a
50–22 record in the regular season.

The team gathered for its annual end-of-season banquet
at a posh Portland hotel. John and Butz had long ago
patched up their differences, and become good friends.
They sat together during the speeches. When Hodge was
announced, everyone in the room rose in a standing ova-

tion. John remained seated until Butz, after repeated nudging, coaxed him to his feet. John gave three weak claps, then sat down.

The next day, the radio brought in the second day's broadcast of the NHL entry draft.

His name was called in the fourth round by the Montreal Canadiens. At last, his dream was coming true.

Downstairs, by a bench, he laid out flat, his eyes fixed on the bar resting on two braces about a foot over his head. He reached up with both hands and rocked it upward, then down and up, repeatedly, in the powerful, rigid strokes of a bench-press motion.

With each repetition, he voiced an acknowledgment to himself, almost chanting, "Fourth round, fourth round . . ."

Chapter Nine

THE MONTREAL FORUM is on St. Catharine Street, a two-minute walk down from the Manoir Lemoine, an apartment-hotel where the Montreal Canadiens house players during training camp.

John walks from the hotel to the Forum and stops for a moment beneath the black, electronic billboard on St. Catharine that posts information about upcoming games.

Two youths, both physically challenged and with speech impediments, wait on the sidewalk as the players trundle in. The boys have pens, hockey cards, and paper.

"Who are you," one asks in a childlike voice.

"I'm John Kordic. I'm going to be playing hockey here," he answers.

They are unfamiliar with the name. They hold out their pens, shy, their arms lifting slowly. John signs his autograph and smiles.

"Thank you, sir."

There is a set of smoked-glass doors through which players and the media enter the building.

Once inside, John must sign in with rink-security personnel, who are also unfamiliar with him. Proudly, he walks through a turnstile, the tradition of the building and the franchise not lost on him.

John heads towards hockey's most famous dressing room and enters.

He glances up and around, taking in the names on the dressing stalls, the famous, inspirational phrase, from the poem "Flanders Field," on the wall (To you from failing hands; we throw the torch; be yours to hold it high). Ever since he was drafted, he wanted to experience this. He sees his own name printed in white block letters on a baby-blue plastic strip that fits into a slot above his dressing stall. For a moment, he feels overwhelming humility.

He had arrived in Montreal in September 1984, with a vague notion of what its franchise expected of him. Dell Wilson, the Canadiens' chief western Canadian scout, who'd orchestrated John's draft selection, told him to work hard and stay focused. The scout had emphasized the latter point.

Wilson warned John about the temptations of big-city night life. While the Forum rises above a quiet, upscale neighborhood surrounding its rear, the main entrances are on St. Catharine and Antoine streets, two streets that pour into the heart of Montreal's vital night life. Sooner or later, most players would make all the regular stops— Thursdays, Winston Churchill's—for a beer. They would easily get past the lineups, and be given the red-carpet treatment. Most patrons were enamored of the Canadiens, so socializing for team members was not a problem. Players periodically dropped into Chez Paree, one of the city's swank exotic dance clubs, or other such establishments, where they were welcomed by staff. Wilson didn't expect John to behave like a monk, but he tried to warn the young hockey player about certain pernicious elements. Wilson's sentiments were reinforced by NHL security personnel, who visited various training camps to discuss drugs, alcohol, gambling, and prostitution.

Wilson informed John that the Canadiens had been looking for an enforcer when they drafted him. Chris Nilan, who had handled the role before Kordic, was also a third-line winger, a skill player. Nilan was to be kept out of the penalty box as much as possible.

The Canadiens also played in the Adams Division, and like every other NHL team, there was a strong emphasis on playing above .500 hockey against other teams in the division. There was an abundance of enforcer types in the division—Jay Miller (Boston Bruins), Torrie Robertson (Hartford Whalers), Shane Churla (Minnesota North

Stars), and Dale Hunter (Quebec Nordiques). Each divisional foe had at least two designated enforcers, save for the Canadiens.

John met the team's management—coach Jean Perron, general manager Serge Savard, and owner Ronald Correy—as well as the trainers and assistant coaches who would direct most of the on-ice drills while the brain trust watched from the bench or on a seat near ice level. Savard was tall, burly, and well-dressed. His hair was still as thick and dark as it had been during his playing days. He smoked a cigar, like Shaw, but there was a rugged authoritativeness that Shaw lacked.

On an almost daily basis, John appeared in Jean Perron's dressing-room office, eagerly asking about the quality of his performance, asking the coach how he could improve his game. Over the course of their discussions, Perron reinforced the merits of hard work and threw in time-honored references about the team, and how great veterans like Larry Robinson, Bobby Smith, and Bob Gainey were close to retiring. Robinson, in particular, had approximately two more years. Out of reverence for the future hall-of-famer, management would allow Robinson to declare his own retirement. Perron believed that the legend's spot on defense would be best filled by John Kordic.

During the first week of training camp, John stepped into Martin Desjardins, another rookie in the camp, with a body-crushing, open-ice check. The thud, and the wind shuddering out of Desjardins's lungs, were audible across the ice. He lay motionless, and while a stretcher was being located, Perron turned to Savard and exclaimed, "I told you, this kid can play." John was proving himself, underscoring Wilson's credibility as a scout, prompting attention from Savard and Perron. The hit was the hardest thrown during the preseason, and would remain so even though John was to be sent back to junior before the regular season arrived. Afterward, the right eyes—Perron's and Savard's—followed John on the ice. The reality of John's ascending to the blue line was marginal, especially with Larry Robinson, Chris Chelios, Gaston Gingras, Rick Green, Mike Lalor, Rick Hayward, and Petr Svoboda already in place. Instead, they had visions of John as a forward.

John continued to play defense through the preseason, but not without incident. Norm Baron, a former American Hockey League (AHL) player was easily the most muscular player in camp. It was inevitable that John and Baron would clash. During one intrasquad scrimmage, the two players collided along the boards. Their sticks came up into each other's faces. In an instant, the gloves dropped.

Baron's strength was incredible. Even when John landed blows, the punches seemed to have little effect. But Baron was slow compared to the rookie, and he failed to deliver an effective counterattack.

Baron challenged John to another round later in the scrimmage. He stunned John with his brute strength, picking him up and slamming him to the ice. Refusing to concede Baron's superior strength, John sprang back on his skates and attacked. His skills took over. Through a rapid series of tugs and grips, he opened a path for his left, and rained more than a dozen blows onto his opponent. Supplemented by several damaging uppercuts, each punch found its mark. The seemingly invincible baron had met his match.

Later that day, Serge Savard complimented John on his scuffle with Baron and told him not to worry, the Canadiens would sign him. Within a week, though, John was on a plane back to Portland.

John's arrival in Portland was welcomed and eagerly anticipated. Most of the Hawks' star players had graduated to the NHL or the AHL, which left a void. For the first time during the franchise's Portland tenure, Shaw had to market a losing team.

Shaw realized the rocky road ahead as early as the fall of 1983 when he made a blockbuster trade, exchanging five veterans for 16-year-old Blaine Chrest, a gifted player from Estevan, Saskatchewan. The trade, originally billed as a 5-for-1, became infamous as a 5-for-0 when Chrest decided to drop junior hockey and pursue his education. One of Shaw's trades, Ray Ferraro, went on to score a league record 108 goals for Brandon.

Because of player turnover, Shaw was forced to retain

three rookie forwards—Dave Archibald, Dave Woodley, and Jeff Finley—and build his offense around them. Just before John returned to Portland, he met with Hodge. They agreed that John would be appointed captain. The rationale was that John was a veteran, a holdover from the Memorial Cup year, and a bona fide star who carried a large enough reputation to dissuade any intimidating challenges to the rookies. The decision also demonstrated the esteem in which management held John—traditionally, the team captaincy was determined by a team vote.

John wore the captain's "C" with pride, but he was a volatile, unpredictable captain.

More than anything, he wanted the "C" on his shoulder to translate into wins, but he lacked the patience necessary to endure the problems of a team that was trying to find itself.

By November 1984, the Hawks were playing miserably, and John tore into the rookies, deriding their talent, making matters worse. He shouted that they would never see a minute on the Canadiens with their current level of play. He dug into himself, trying to will success out of his own play. He began solo missions, rink-long rushes with the puck, like Bobby Orr. And in the process, he abandoned his own duties at the blue line.

Hodge and Shaw were approached by some rookies with complaints about John's incompetence as team captain. Both men realized the captaincy was a recipe for disaster if John's attitude didn't change. They'd seen signs of John's cockiness a year earlier, when Hodge had ordered him to leave practice because of offensive comments the young player had made. Now that he was captain, John openly defied his coach. In one game during a woeful road trip in November 1984, his frustration at the team's inability to execute simple breakouts boiled over. He froze the puck in his own zone, almost incurring a penalty for delaying the game. Then he skated over to the bench and exchanged words with Shaw. He was promptly benched.

Hodge began to bench John for shifts, then periods. He no longer attempted to stickhandle the issue. In a mid-

November story in *The Oregonian,* Hodge said, "John continues to make the same mistake over and over again, and it's creating a lot of problems in our own zone." In the same story, John retorted, "I know I played bad in the first period, and maybe I try to do too much, but I'm not doing it for myself. I'm trying to help out the hockey club. I want to win, and maybe I want to do too much to win. Because I'm older and have been around more, I guess I try to do more."

Dell Wilson and Doug Robinson—scouts for the Canadiens—followed John through the disastrous road trip, which carried the Hawks on painfully long bus trips across the Prairies. Shaw wanted John to step up the physical side of his game, which meant fighting the opposition's tough guy to set an example for his own team. Shaw approached Wilson, explaining that his efforts to communicate with John had failed. Wilson and Robinson spoke with John in the hotel, and the next day, Kordic squared off in a bruising bout with Saskatoon's Randy Hoffart. The Hawks won the game 8–2.

But Shaw had seen enough. Before the road trip was over, he floated a rumor about John's being available for the right trade. Soon after, he dispensed with reticence on Dean Vrooman's radio show, and exclaimed, "Something has to be done with John Kordic on this team."

Shaw was further aggravated by reports that John was breaking curfew back in Portland. John loved his billet, the Olsons, but after the obligatory wait in his room to answer the phone, he would often slip out a window and meet other players and friends downtown. Shaw was also troubled by some of the younger players' idolization of John. One of them, Troy Arnt, even went so far as to get the same haircut as Kordic and mimic his hero's behavior. There was no doubt about it—John and Shaw were on a collision course.

John's rebelliousness surfaced again after a home game against Kamloops, when the Blazers' team bus was loaded before it crept out of town. Kamloops' coach Ken "Hitch" Hitchcock, who'd sold John a pair of skates during the young player's midget days in Edmonton, had taken his regular seat at the front of the bus, when he was disturbed by incessant laughter from his players. He went to investigate and marched down the aisle. The laughter waned as he approached the rear of the bus, where the toilet was located. He opened the door, and found John sitting on the commode, grinning. "C'mon, Hitch, trade for me, get me the fuck outta here," John said. Hitchcock shook his head, then ordered the bus driver back to Portland.

On December 3, 1984, Hodge summoned John to his office to tell him he'd been traded to Brandon.

John, however, was not going to go quietly. Refusing to report to Brandon, he stomped out of Hodge's office.

After more than two years of hard work, John felt betrayed. Shaw arranged a subtext to the trade, involving Seattle in a three-way deal which would see Brandon receive two other players and John play for the Breakers. When called upon to comment, Shaw told the media he'd secured Seattle as a personal favor to John. Ultimately, the deal proved to be one of the best in Portland history. The Hawks received Dennis Holland and Jim Agnew. Agnew went on to captain the 1985–86 team, and became one of the franchise's top players.

Shaw also met with disapproval from the Olsons. After a heated exchange with Chuck and Barb Olson in which he denigrated John, he threw up his hands in frustration and exclaimed, "Who the hell is John Kordic anyway?" The following spring at the annual billets barbecue, every billet contract with the Hawks was renewed, except for the Olsons.

John agreed to report to Seattle, and instantly became a fan favorite. Shaw was booed and yelled at during Portland's first game after the trade. Several fans sat with brown paper bags over their heads, which had "R.I.P. No. 4" scribbled on them. Attendance fell off dramatically. In three games following the trade, the Hawks, who were averaging 4,476 fans per game, drew 2,375, 3,010, and 2,229, respectively.

John had told *The Oregonian* he wanted to play in the West Division so that he could face the Hawks as many times as possible. His first game back he was wearing number 9, and scored a goal and two assists despite his team's loss. During the pregame warm-ups, John talked with fans near the corner boards, boasting he was going to thrash several star Hawks. At the beginning of the game, he was cheered by the Portland fans, but they grew silent after he delivered a hard hit on star defenseman Glenn Wesley. Later, he had Wesley lined up again, but Wesley saw him and stopped short of the collision point. John fired a cross-check into Wesley anyway and challenged him to drop his gloves. Wesley skated away, and the fans began to boo every time John touched the puck.

Although he was no longer a hero in Portland, Seattle fans began a love affair with John after only his first fight. They quickly changed the signs that read "How do you spell goon: K-O-R-D-I-C," to "this is Kordic Country."

When John left Portland, after 25 games, he had six goals and 25 assists. He went on to finish the season in Seattle with another 17 goals and 36 assists, his best totals in junior. In April 1985, he was named to the WHL's second all-star team, behind Glenn Wesley and Wendel Clark.

Chapter Ten

AFTER FINISHING his junior career in Seattle, John joined the Canadiens' AHL affiliate in Sherbrooke, Quebec, for the team's AHL play-off run. He appeared in four games, his presence coinciding with an incredible late-season drive in which Sherbrooke edged the Baltimore Skipjacks for the Calder Cup.

Sherbrooke's fairy-tale rise to stardom gelled as soon as the team's band of talented players found a groove and stayed with it. The team, anchored by Patrick Roy in goal, included an impressive cast of future NHL debutants: Stephane Richer, Mike Keane, Brian Skrudland, Mike Lalor, Gaston Gingras, Rick Natress, Steven Fletcher, Thomas Rundqvist, and Claude Lemieux. They won 27 of their final 34 games, and beat the Adirondack Red Wings on the last game of the season—a do-or-die affair for the play-off aspirations of both teams.

The Canadiens recalled John from Sherbrooke, Quebec, in a patent piece of roster tuning for the play-off grind. There was no mistaking, or apologizing, for the presence of an enforcer when the postseason came.

By March 1985, John's reputation was embellished by further reports about his wild side, his excessive drinking, and hair-trigger temper, which sometimes saw him take swings at bar patrons. These tendencies had been fostered in Portland and Seattle, but now that he was under the aegis of the Montreal organization, there had to be controls.

The following season, on an unofficial ordinance from coach Pierre Creamer, Steven Fletcher acted as John's watchdog. Fletcher had fought with John at previous Montreal training camps and was often approached to step in when John was threatening to slug it out with some local. As belligerent as he was, John was also inordinately likable, and Fletcher grew to like and care a great deal for him.

At six foot one and 205 pounds, with 238 penalty minutes to his "credit," John was one of the AHL's most talked-about enforcers. He came to understand the vicissitudes of being an enforcer as he squared off against foes far bigger and tougher than those he had dominated in junior. He proved his mettle against Val James of the St. Catharines Saints and Torrie Robertson of the Binghampton Whalers, both of whom bore the league standard in strength, intimidation, and just plain nastiness. During warm-ups, St. Catharines coach John Brophy often had Val James stand menacingly, chest bare and arms crossed, within sight of an opposing team. John readily absorbed such tactics.

At the time, in April 1986, John was summoned to Montreal, Fletcher was spreading himself thin trying to cover John's galloping transgressions. Fletcher was finding it increasingly difficult to decide when to confront John, and when to turn a blind eye. In one instance, when he discovered from his wife that John had propositioned her, he refused to dignify John's behavior with a reaction. Another time, against his better judgment, he followed John to a bar out on a highway leading out of Sherbrooke, at the cutoff to Lennoxville. Fletcher knew the crowd was trouble—Hells Angels trafficked cocaine there. The bar itself drew national media attention a short time later when the bodies of several suspected Hells Angels were recovered from the bottom of the St. Lawrence River. They had been chain-wrapped in brick-laden sleeping bags—the apparent retribution for skimming coke profits. John's love of the night life had not yet led him into the world of cocaine. At the time, Fletcher did not know that the RCMP had undertaken an investigation of the bar, and that John's name would appear on the organization's intelligence reports as a person associating with the biker element.

John faced coach Jean Perron on the eve of the 1985–86 Stanley Cup play-offs. Alone with Perron, John's eyes were deep, penetrating in their blackness. Yet, when he spoke, there was an urgency to impress the older man. He had been recalled earlier in the season, on a two-game stint in January during which he'd scored against the New York Rangers for his first NHL goal. He sent the puck home, where Ivan built a special plaque for it and hung it in the family room. Perron, in his rookie season as head coach in Montreal, also felt an urgency. He was under pressure to prove his effectiveness. There was great reverence for the Stanley Cup–winning coaches in Montreal: Bowman, Blake, Hart, Irvin. Perron wanted to measure up.

"You can't drop the gloves and fight everybody," Perron continued. "If someone makes a bad check on one of our little guys, one of our best players, you know, this guy can't do that anymore. You gotta talk to him, you talk to him and you tell him you know, you give him a first warning, and then if he goes back again at our best players, you have to react.

"But you know, I don't want you to go and drop the gloves for nothing, cause that's a stupid penalty in my book."

"I just want to play . . . I want the ice time," John said. "I want to be out there and contribute. I won't let you down."

Perron decided not to use John on defense. John had never developed the lateral movement required of a big-league defenseman. The Canadiens blue line was virtually sewn up in the meantime. Perron broke the news that John would be assigned to right wing for the Stanley Cup run.

"Take care of your position," Perron said. "Take care of your own zone, and don't hang on to the puck. When you reach the red line and you don't see anybody open, you dump the puck, dump on the far wing side, you know, ready to get it back. You play smart, and you stay the third man into the zone."

"No problem, I'll do anything you like," John said.

Perron sequestered the team in a hotel on an island just off the Lafontaine Bridge. He wanted his team focused. At this hotel, all distractions—wives, friends, bars, the press—were out. As the play-offs wore on, the players grew to loathe the place, dubbing the island "Alcatraz."

The Canadiens opened the play-offs in nightmarish fashion. They were paired against the Boston Bruins in a best-of-three Adams Division semifinal, and the Bruins set an overwhelming pace in the first period. They outshot Montreal 11–7, and there was only Patrick Roy to thank for a 0–0 score. The Canadiens were shell shocked.

In the intermission, Perron, walking through the dressing room to his office, was stopped dead by Bob Gainey's exclamation, "Coach, what are we gonna do, for chrissake."

"Two things," he said.

"First of all, shorter shifts . . . Second, discipline, and that means you, Chris Nilan."

Perron felt Nilan's performance was shadowed by the player's preoccupation with body checking, slashing, and shoving every Bruin within reach. As assistant coach with the Canadiens a year before, Perron had seen the same tendency in Nilan. They'd discussed it through the regular season, and Perron felt they had reached an agreement. Although Perron understood that it was natural for Nilan, who came from Boston, to react emotionally when the Canadiens played the Bruins, the coach would not accept aberrant behavior, not for any reason.

"Chris, you're gonna play hockey, you're not gonna run everybody. John is going to do the fighting if we have to."

The Canadiens went on to score three goals in the second period, and ultimately sweep the Bruins in three straight games.

A significant portion of Perron's postseason brain trust was now invested in a 21-year-old enforcer who couldn't technically be called a rookie. John was a raw recruit, a call-up with only five NHL games under his belt. But Perron understood a calculated risk. In John he saw enough mettle and spirit to see him through the toughest games.

Kordic was strong and fit. He had stamina and strength when fighting and could throw punches equally well with both hands—a style not familiar to most NHL enforcers of the time.

John carved out a niche against Jay Miller, the Bruins' celebrated scrapper. After one nationally televised beating by John, Miller, unnerved and in stick-swinging frustration, stormed down the corridor to the dressing room, where he attempted to boot the door open with his skate. Instead, his blades shot out from under him, and in a comical, memorable moment, he ended up on his derriere, while the cameras were still rolling. John was fond of referring to their bouts as "Miller Time."

Perron told the media that John was doing a man's job, and John continued to play that role in series wins over the Hartford Whalers and New York Rangers. The coach found ways to keep John in every game, even if it meant not dressing defenseman Petr Svoboda, the 1984 first-round pick. He told himself he would go with six defensemen instead of seven, and if one of the blue liners was injured, he would insert John in the vacancy. Perron speculated that he may not have come to the Stanley Cup final without John in his lineup.

John busily polished his style. After each successful bout, he stood over his opponents, the triumphant pugilist, then skated away and kissed his fists. A powerful image, Kordic in the limelight. It intoxicated him—the sound of 17,000 fans in the Forum chanting, "Kordic! Kordic! Kordic!"

Perron used John sparingly in the final against the Calgary Flames. The need for a physical presence presented itself only once, in the conclusion to game four in Calgary, when a bench-clearing brawl was anticlimactic to a Canadiens 1–0 win. What happened was this: The Flames were ripe to scuttle any victory by the Canadiens. They had been prodded by Claude Lemieux, who specialized in subtle holds, slashes, and cheap shots that frustrated opponents. It was more than the Flames could take when Lemieux scored the game's lone goal, which was also his tenth of the postseason, and led all play-off scorers. By the

final whistle, the Flames were entirely unnerved. The result
was a free-for-all which netted a total fine of $42,000 for
both teams. Calgary cocaptain Jim Peplinski was asked the
next day about the fines, and displayed his finger, which
Lemieux had apparently gnawed on during the nastiness.
"Did they say anything about cannibalism?" he quipped.

On Saturday, May 24, 1986, the game following the
1–0 win, the Canadiens clinched the Stanley Cup with a
4–3 win in Calgary. There were yelps of joy from the victorious players above the din of the disappointed Calgary
crowd. The players were among the few people in hockey
who believed the Canadiens could actually walk away
with the championship.

John was on the ice, having shared in the tradition of
holding the Stanley Cup overhead during a victory lap,
when a microphone was put in front of him. He was asked
for a reaction. "Oh, this is the best fuckin' thing that's ever
happened to me, I can't fuckin' believe it . . ." he said.
Later, in an interview with the *Edmonton Journal,* he said
he was the "luckiest guy on earth . . . first the Memorial
Cup, then the Calder Cup, now the Stanley Cup. I think
I'll go out and play the lottery next."

A picture: In the dressing room, Ivan next to John.
Laughter between them, champagne being poured over
John's head, John running his fingers through his hair to
primp it back into shape. In his undershirt, his hockey
pants still on, John sitting on a table next to the cup, looking out into the room. Ivan on the other side, nearest the
camera, looking at it, his face flushed with laughter. They
were captured together that way, for posterity.

Montreal opened like a playground for the players in the
wake of the team's championship win. People began to see
John regularly in the bars on Crescent Street. He called
Fletcher to join him in the celebrating, and to accompany
him on a team trip to the Bahamas.

Just before their departure, the two men were sitting in
the outdoor patio of Winston Churchill's. The subject
came up of what John would do for an encore.

"I'll be back, they told me I'd be back . . ."

"Who's they, Johnny?"

"Ah, you know, management . . . they want me to be the biggest guy in the league when I come back, bigger than Probert or any of them. It's gonna be wild."

Chapter Eleven

IT WAS SUMMER 1986. John was on leave from the Canadiens, cruising the streets of Edmonton with his friend, Tim. It was also the summer he met blond, blue-eyed, vivacious Sandy Bernard. Within a month of meeting each other, John and Sandy were seeing each other every day. Almost immediately after he'd met her, John told Sandy she wasn't like the girls he had met in Montreal. They were so materialistic, he said, while she was down-to-earth. Sandy hadn't known him long enough to see past what appeared to be a routine come-on.

In Seattle, before he left to join Sherbrooke, he had similar feelings for a girl he'd met after a game. When he left Seattle for the last time, he cried for her. It was an incongruous sight, an enforcer, brash and cocky, reduced to showing his more tender emotions. He asked everyone who'd witnessed this vulnerable side of him not to tell anyone what they'd seen. Glimpses of that rare emotion surfaced when John brought children home for one of Regina's generous feedings. "Kids like you for you," he was fond of saying.

In 1986, on the July long weekend, John drove Sandy to her friend's house in west Edmonton. She and her girl-friend were going to the annual Peach Festival in Penticton, British Columbia, and he wasn't invited.

Not prepared to take no for an answer, John whined and cajoled until Sandy agreed to meet him there.

Immediately, John was at a travel agency, booking a

flight. He was in British Columbia the next day, waiting for Sandy at a small airport. She was over an hour late, and John didn't take well to waiting.

Sandy and her friend finally pulled up to the sidewalk by the lobby entrance, and honked their horn for John. It was getting late, and they were due in Kelowna for a private party at one of the town's trendy waterfront bars.

Kelowna was a hotbed for vacationing hockey players. Several players ran or participated in local hockey schools, while some retired players opened restaurant/bars there. At any party that mattered around town, they were usually there.

At the hotel, Sandy's friends began drawing lines of cocaine in the washroom. John saw them leaning in, a twenty-dollar bill rolled up like a straw, and knew what they were up to. He was enraged. Sandy did her best to deflect his fury, and to reassure her friends, who were intimidated by John's anger. He'd reacted similarly in Portland when his roommate had continued to smoke marijuana, even though John had shown his disapproval. He'd told the Olsons that he couldn't live under the same roof as a "druggie."

Later, John noticed Sandy trying to discourage the advances of a man he had never seen before. The man kept asking Sandy to go out for a drive. John, his attitude already iced by the previous delays, stood squarely in front of the man's face.

"Go mind your own business . . ." the man said, blandly.

"This *is* my business."

In a matter of seconds, several bouncers and hockey players had converged on John. It took seven of them to get him out to the parking lot. Greg Adams, of the Vancouver Canucks, and several other NHL players helped restore John to a calmer state.

When Sandy and John returned to Edmonton, they were still a couple—more so than before. She admired his convictions, and understood that it was this, as well as his fiery nature, that attracted him to her. She learned that under the tough exterior was vulnerability. She learned that John was unique, and the sight of his tears began to make more sense to her.

When John came back to Edmonton from Montreal, he brought with him a new Canadiens jacket for Ivan.

John joined his father at Ivan's employer's barbecue. There were handshakes and autographs, smiles and adulation. John gave a personally autographed Canadiens jersey to Ivan's boss at Artek, a furniture manufacturer with an international reputation for filling high-dollar custom orders.

Ivan was enjoying a considerable measure of success as a cabinet maker, working on projects for Wayne Gretzky, Bloomingdales, and clients in Hollywood.

John attended masses given by Father Anthony Juric. He maintained his Catholic faith through intermittent visits to the church, usually for Sunday services. He was out most nights with friends, barhopping, or seeing Sandy. He had become friends with the owner at Barry T's, a suburban nightclub popular with some of the Edmonton Oilers and other Edmonton athletes. Throughout the summer, he was invited to act as a guest bartender.

In August, John was asked to act as a guest instructor at some of the better hockey schools around town. The schools helped him regain his skating legs. At the time, however, his focus was a heavy bodybuilding program.

John had become a member at Titan's gym, a mecca for Edmonton bodybuilders. He befriended the owner, a man he would eventually share an apartment with. The man was known in bodybuilding circles as a steroid guru: someone who took them as well as supplied them. John saw the spectacle of his friend's body in workouts, then tried to emulate it with his own intense workouts.

John's initiation into the bodybuilding culture afforded him lessons in steroid use. Steroids are primarily muscle builders, helping the muscles recover and grow more rapidly than normal. Some of these drugs, like a substance called Winstrol V, are labeled: For Veterinarian Use Only. Winstrol V produces a host of side effects—including increased aggressiveness—that most users never take seriously. Equipoise, far less riskier in terms of side effects, is referred to as the cleanest of the commonly used steroids. It has the same effect as Ventipullum, or Clenbuterol, which reduces water retention and increases oxygen capacity in the cells. Both are popular with bodybuilders and strippers since the results gained are a tighter skin, or "thin" skin, which helps emphasize the deeply "cut" look serious bodybuilders strive for, or a women's breasts or leg muscles. Steroid users also swallow tablespoonfuls of baking soda. This practice is popular with some long-distance runners who ingest it to break down painful lactic acid buildup. Moreover, the presence of baking soda in the urine specimen of a person undergoing a drug test breaks down the test indicators, producing a cloudy result.

Before the end of August, John was back at the Tomahawk Hockey School as a guest instructor. It was evident by then that his physique had made improbable muscle gains.

Bill Laforge was sitting in his office at the Enoch arena, on the phone with his wife. He looked up as John entered, then returned to his phone conversation. There was a thud on the corner of his desk. John had slammed his elbow down, his forearm pointed straight into the air. He wanted to arm wrestle.

After hanging up with his wife, Laforge obliged him, having done so in the past without once losing. When they locked grips, though, Laforge felt an incredible hardness in John, something he had never before felt. He looked at John, gamely, bracing himself for a struggle. When they both let loose with the pull, there was no struggle. John overpowered him with ease, then plowed the back of his wrist into the desk.

John rose from the desk, raising his hands in the air like a boxing champion, then strode off to the rear of the arena where the weight room was.

Laforge shook his head in disbelief, laughed to himself, then went back to his paperwork and phone calls.

Several minutes later, he heard laughter outside his door. Several youths were talking about John.

"You should see this guy lifting weights down there."

Laforge came into the room just as John, sweating and

wrapped in a towel, was making his way to the sauna. He saw an implausibly narrow waist and a giant, V-tapered back. He also saw patches of acne on John's skin. A sudden rush of disappointment overcame him.

"Tell me you're not doing what I think you're doing," he said to John.

"What do you mean?"

"You know, the steroid stuff. I wouldn't have guessed it, but look at ya . . . Tell me you're not doing it."

John was evasive. But later, as Laforge stood next to John's car, he couldn't help noticing the open trunk and gym bag in which he saw a number of tiny bottles with unfamiliar names and labels.

"There are easier ways to kill yourself, John," he said.

"I've gotta be strong, Coach. I've gotta be because the kids are coming up and I've gotta be stronger than they are."

"You're just a kid yourself."

John changed the subject. He joked for a moment, talked about an upcoming intrasquad game at the school, told Laforge that training camp was less than two weeks away.

Then, with a push from his arm, the trunk swooshed shut, and John slipped into the driver's seat. He said goodbye, and left Laforge watching him pull out of the parking lot.

Chapter Twelve

CHRIS NILAN appeared at the players' bench half-dressed and with no skates on.

He told John to get off the ice and report to the dressing room, the coach wanted him.

"What the fuck is going on, you guys," John barked, his voice echoing in the empty corridor leading to the dressing-room door. Nilan had disappeared and the dressing room was open, and strangely silent. Suddenly, it hit him. In the training camp of 1986–87, rookies were skating around with a full head of hair one day, then suddenly appearing shaved to the skull the next. He sat down at his locker, not knowing whether to laugh or complain, and began removing his skates.

A voice called him into the trainers' room, adjacent to the locker room. He walked in the room barefoot, wearing a short-sleeve undershirt. He was told to sit down on a table in the middle of the room. He did as he was told. A cloth was wrapped around his head, covering his eyes. He heard players filing in, and laughter. Hands on him now, he is made to lie back. Then tape, on his hands and legs.

He heard first the buzz of barber's clippers, then felt the cool steeliness as the first stroke came up behind his ear. Stay still, he was told, the more he moved the worse it would look. He howled obscenities. Hands on his head, holding him down, and laughter, encouragement, and one-liners. Rambo's pissed, they said. Rambo was the nickname he was tagged with in the Stanley Cup play-offs. His arms rocked, the tape restraints groaned. He was seething. Then scissors, cutting the tape, and everyone scattering in laughter.

He sat up instantly, shredding the remainder of the tape around his legs, and pulling off the blindfold. Everyone was back in the dressing room. Then he saw it; the hair around his ears, sides of his head, back of his head, all gone. Only a thin strip running from front to back along the top of his head remained. They'd given him a Mohawk.

In the next couple of days, his picture appeared in the paper: he was standing between Shane Corson and Dave Malley. All three were sporting their new haircuts.

Corson and Mike Lalor were going to share a flat with John on Nunn's Island. John had fought with Corson at the outset of camp, a brutal confrontation in which Corson more than held his own. John had been livid when the decision went to Corson. Having inherited the team's "heavyweight" title, he could not allow any challengers. He lunged at Corson a second time, carrying the feud into the corridor, until Nilan and Guy Carboneau stepped in to separate them. It was ugly, and some of his teammates began to wonder why Kordic reacted so violently. Ironically, Corson and John benefited from the fight. Corson wound up making the team, in part because management approved of his willingness to fight John, concluding he was tough enough for the NHL. As for John, he may have lost a degree of respect among the players, but he was now the standard of toughness against which all other rookies were measured. John phoned his parents once camp broke to tell them he was a Montreal Canadien.

Early in the season, he came to Edmonton for a game against the Oilers. It was the perfect setting, he decided, to show his mettle as an enforcer. He knew he would be sent out against Kevin McClelland, the Oilers' tough guy.

When they met, the fight between John and McClelland was spectacular. Rod Phillips, the radio voice of the Oilers, delivered the play-by-play: "Those two guys are tough, I'm talking tough . . . McClelland banging away with left hands, and *ohhhhh*, Kornic [sic] coming back now . . ."

In spite of his having mispronounced John's surname, Phillips insisted it was the best fight he'd seen in ten years. Word of the go-around eventually reached Nutley, New Jersey, prompting fight-tape guru Sandy Vigilante to ask for a copy. The game, however, hadn't been televised. Vigilante, who stocks several thousand tapes and creates professional-quality videos for many of hockey's top enforcers, was adamant about getting a taped copy of the fight. A version was eventually taken from team-video footage of the game.

John had earned a spot on the roster, and with it the spoils of a professional athlete's lifestyle. In the heady aftermath of the Stanley Cup celebration, John had met Michel Labonte, a well-known Montreal kick boxer who, in the late 1970s, was ranked in the top ten in the world. Labonte owned a bar named L'arnaque II, which loosely translated into English, means "The Sting." Many players were patrons at Labonte's bar, which worried Canadiens' management. Labonte also worked at Molson Breweries, the beer-manufacturing giant and principal shareholder on the Canadiens' board of governors. In his overalls, he loaded trucks like hundreds of other blue-collar wage earners. His club, though, was located in St. Leonard's, Montreal's famous Italian district, where members of the underworld came to socialize. It was the type of scene that earned Labonte the reputation of being "well-connected."

John came to roost regularly at L'arnaque II. Labonte befriended John, and like most people who met the young hockey player, he found it hard to say no to anything John asked for. For the most part, John's relationship with his roommates, Corson and Lalor, was going smoothly. But when John needed his own space, there was always a room for him at Labonte's apartment. John ingratiated himself with many of the patrons at the bar, passing them tickets to games, and posing for pictures, like a movie star.

John also made the rounds of Montreal's hotter strip clubs. Many women were seduced by the stories they'd read about him in the papers, intrigued by his reputation, the crowds chanting his name, the clips of him kissing his fists. In their rooms, or in hotels, he explored exotic and dangerous things. John saw himself as a sexual conqueror, adventurous, invincible.

John was in the washroom of a bar with a friend, a man well known in organized-crime circles, who wore lavish clothes and expensive jewelry.

"John, have you met my friend?" John shook hands with a second man. He noticed a plastic baggie, open, lying on the black marble counter. A white powder had been drawn in a thin line about three inches long.

"You never done this shit before, bro . . . Oh, we got a virgin here, we got a fuckin' rookie."

"In here, you guys are crazy, you're doing that in here?" John said.

The man leaned over. He had a twenty-dollar bill rolled up tightly, like a straw. He put the bill at one end of the line. He brought his nostril over the other end of the bill. In one fluid motion, he ran it down the length of the line, inhaling hard. The powder disappeared.

"You want one?" the man asked John.

Deftly, quickly, he had prepared another line. John had always said no in the past, but he didn't want to appear anything less than his own man before his friend.

"Fuck it," he said, and bent over.

When he came up, it didn't feel like anything. The inside of his nose was numb. His nose hairs felt burned away. He looked in the mirror to check. He stuck his finger in his nose. His friend laughed.

The man gave John the rest of the bag, a freebie, along with a macabre blessing that the gesture was a personal favor. John thought of flushing it down the toilet, but he remembered how fashionable the substance was with the girls he knew. He tucked it into his pocket, like a talisman.

The man resurfaced at strip clubs and bars that John frequented. But there were no more freebies.

· · · ·

John had money to spend. Before the 1986–87 season began, the Canadiens had signed him to a three-year deal—two years plus an option year—that would give him an annual salary of $150,000, on par with the average NHL salary at the time. Soon, a lot of men and women came looking for him, looking to make friends.

As the season wore on, John made friends with people who did lines with him. They were people he could call, from anywhere in the city, at any time, people who enlivened his life. When Sandy came to visit, she was impressed with the fuss people made over John in nightclubs. He was always glad to sign autographs, the adulation providing a natural high he fed on more than the drug. His appetite for cocaine, however, was becoming more and more insatiable.

Labonte condoned John's behavior. Like many who happened into John's life, he felt a kinship with him. John was always welcome at the Labontes. Labonte also brought John to Daniel Harvey's, a house on West Island well known for helping substance abusers. He had brought two other players there in the past; both defeated their habits. He dropped John off twice, for very short periods; no results.

Eventually, Labonte's reputation and business suffered as the rumors of John's drug use circulated. Players who had regularly patronized L'arnaque II—Nilan, Malley, Lalor, Richer, Chelios, and Greene—stopped coming. Labonte later learned that he had been named as John's pusher. He was told that the Canadiens, after seeking advice from the police and high-profile insiders who associated with the players, had declared his club off limits to players.

Throughout the season, rumors about John's—and other players'—lifestyles spread. The Montreal media speculated wildly about Richer's sexual orientation. There was never anything to substantiate these reports, but the insinuations were damaging nonetheless. Gossip about the drinking and fighting exploits of Corson and Chelios in Montreal night spots also spread like wildfire. And of course, John's dark side fueled the gossip mills. Respect for John dwindled among the players, especially when he contracted a sexually transmitted disease. Perron, suspicious that John was not the only player so afflicted, ordered his trainers to use triple of whatever they were using to purify the water in the team whirlpool.

Perron called John to his office on several occasions in the early stages of the season. He had concluded that John was taking steroids after seeing the player's implausible muscle gains. Perron had been impressed with John's skills four months earlier during the Stanley Cup. His skating was ordinary, but his shot was excellent; he could pass and handle the puck as well as some of the team's regular wingers. John's new bulk, however, dulled his former edge. He lost his position in the starting lines, and wound up part of the overflow of players who stayed in game shape but played irregularly. Throughout the NHL there were similar players, fringe players. They were dubbed "Black Aces" because they wore black jerseys in practice. After the starters left the ice, they remained on the ice. Perron left his aces to Jacques Laperriere, whose job it was to drill and skate them so hard they would strive to get back into the lineup.

What concerned Perron were the rumors of John's cocaine use. He confronted the hockey player, but got nowhere. Kordic denied everything. Perron took his concerns to Savard, who, like Perron, had also heard the rumors.

Before the season reached midpoint, John was assigned to Sherbrooke. He returned to his locker in despair.

The demotion was, in effect, a conditioning stint, and John was recalled within two weeks. Wanting to show he belonged, he fought more wildly than ever. After one vicious battering, in which he flurried blows off Richard Zemlak's helmet and injured his hand, he curtsied to Quebec coach Michel Bergeron and blew kisses to the players on the bench.

Perron continued to use John as an enforcer, and so, the irregular ice time continued, as well. John's bitterness turned to rage. He stormed into Perron's office, ranting, grabbing the coach's heavy wood-and-metal desk. John shook it violently, moving it like matchwood. Perron would have none of John's tirades and threw him out. John's ice time was not increased.

A few days after John's tirade in Perron's office, a story appeared in *La Presse,* a sensational story full of derogatory comments from John about how the coach mismanaged him.

This prompted another meeting in Perron's office.

"John, you are not going to start going to the press every time you are not happy . . . you are going to come to me." Perron said. Then he handed him a scrap of paper, upon which was written: "Your importance on this hockey club is not related to your ice time—it's not how much you play, it's what you do for the club."

Afterward, rumors circulated in media circles that in his rage over reduced ice time, John had threatened to harm Perron and his family. The media readily attributed his extreme behavior to steroid use, and traded the hockey player's "Rambo" nickname in favor of a new designation—"The Incredible Hulk."

Reporters never witnessed John in a pregame dressing room, or between periods. During those times, he engaged in a ritual practiced by many enforcers. He would smooth-slick gobs of vaseline around his eyes and cheeks, something boxers commonly did. His fingers and wrists were taped, and fit into specially tailored gloves, which were shortened so they could be shucked off quickly in the event of a scrap. He would also tie his jersey to his hockey pants with skate laces to prevent it from being pulled up over his head. All the while, he focused on his role, and on the opposition's tough guys. Most of the NHL enforcers were still a mystery to him.

Even with dozens of fights to his career credit, the night before each game, Kordic had trouble sleeping. He was alone when he stepped onto the ice. No one could understand the fear and uncertainty unless they experienced it themselves. He came prepared to play—and to wage war. Then, the disappointment—of not playing unless he was called upon to fill the role of an enforcer—created stress and anguish. While most players sat between periods, he paced, struck a wall or partition with his fist, or uttered obscenities.

One day, after a Canadiens win, Perron noticed John talking on the telephone inside the trainers room. He had seen John there before, leaning over the carapace, his arm draped over the top edge. Sometimes, John would have tears in his eyes, and he knew John was talking to his father. This time, again, John was crying.

"John, what's the matter, we won the game, why are you crying?"

"I just got shit from my dad, he doesn't like the way I am playing."

"You can talk to your dad, I met your dad, he is a good man."

Perron was concerned, but also curious. He never saw John yell into the phone on such occasions. His head was always just below his outstretched arm, he was always leaning in, face close to the phone. Sometimes he would turn to see where the other players were. His voice was always low, subdued.

"My dad's like my idol, but he never played the game. He doesn't want me to do what I'm doing. I don't know how to tell him. He pushed me in sports, and for that I'll remember him for the rest of my life . . . you know, for what he did, because if I'm playing the game, it's because of him."

Perron left John, with a mental note to periodically check with John on his relationship with his father. He recalled meeting Ivan in the Stanley Cup play-offs. He was struck by the fact that Ivan was so much smaller, yet could command enormous respect from the intimidating John Kordic.

He also recalled Ivan's manners, and judged him to be a man with deep rooted honor and morals. Ivan had told Jean: "Mr. Perron, if you have any problem with John, tell me, give me a call. I want my son to be respectful, I want him to be a good person. In life it's important to be a good person."

Chapter Thirteen

POULIN TARDIFF and his family live in a dream home overlooking a lake in the picturesque northern district of Montreal.

All around, there are trees, shrubs, and wonderfully manicured lawns and gardens. In the winter, the Tardiff children play hockey on the frozen surface of the lake, just across the street and down a small embankment.

Tardiff met John at a Canadiens golf tournament in the late summer of 1987. As owner and president of Bestar, an office furniture manufacturer considered one of the top 10 companies of its type in Canada, he was often invited to team functions, where friends, sponsors, and the media mingled with the players.

Poulin also dropped by the Forum for games and practices—the privilege of playing golf in the right circles. At one practice, Guy Carboneau indicated to Tardiff that John needed a place to stay. John was headed into his second full year with the Canadiens, and wanted to terminate his living arrangement with Corson and Lalor. Before the end of the day, Tardiff brought John home to meet his wife, Gabby, and their sons Martin and Simon. John soon took up residence in an upper-floor unit of the Tardiff house.

Before the previous season had ended, a letter from Edmonton arrived at the Canadiens office. In it was a plea from the Kordic family: you are paying our son $150,000 a year and he is spending it on cocaine, please watch out for him.

One winter morning, Poulin noticed John standing at the living-room window, peering out at the neighborhood kids who were flashing up and down on the lake, making plays and celebrating goals.

As wild as John's night life had become, he often found himself alone, and shy of strangers who might shun him as the "goon" of the Montreal Canadiens—a term the media often used to refer to him. He had drifted away from Corson and Lalor, partly because they were content to confine their partying to the Crescent Street bars, while he ventured, alone, to the north-end strip joints, where his friends worked. Many nights, though, he remained in his bedroom surfing the movie channels on his giant-screen television. He knew half the team's players had little respect for him. By now, the feeling was mutual. They accepted his devotion to his role as team enforcer, but the consensus was that he led a debauched lifestyle, which only widened the distance between John and his teammates.

"John, why don't you go out and join Martin, maybe get some fresh air," Poulin said.

"Ah, I don't have my skates here . . . they probably wouldn't want me anyways."

He began to turn some of his attention to the disabled kids outside the Forum. He took them to lunch, for sodas and ice cream. He often dropped in to the café behind the arena, with them in tow. On one occasion, Bob Probert was sitting inside with his lawyer Patrick Ducharme, waiting for an order. Ducharme had been asked by the Red Wings to accompany the team on road trips, to help keep Probert out of trouble. John, instantly recognizing the NHL's widely acclaimed number-one enforcer, walked by and said, "Hi Bob, how's it goin', hope you have a good game tonight." Probert never raised his head, never took his eyes off his coffee cup. When John left, Ducharme wondered why his client behaved so poorly. "He just doesn't want to fuckin' fight me tonight," Probert snorted.

"Here, you can wear these," Poulin said, handing John a pair of knee-high fishing boots.

John pondered them for a moment, clearly unimpressed by the cumbersome, unfashionable footwear. But he recognized Tardiff's gesture for what it was, and put on the clumsy boots.

In the garage, the Tardiffs kept several old hockey sticks. Most of them were cracked, the tape weathered and frilled, or the bottom edge of the blade ragged from games on the street. John grabbed one, shabby and small for his six-foot-one, 210-pound frame, and headed out to the ice and the boys flashing by on skates.

John's Canadiens' jacket was like a siren, and Martin and all his friends came running. When Martin had mentioned the exciting news that a hockey player would be staying with his family, the neighborhood kids had never imagined him skating on the lake with them. None of them noticed the boots.

John ran awkwardly on the ice, and the boots made a groaning noise when he slid to a stop. Many of the players, awestruck, waited for him to pass the puck when it was on his stick. When they challenged him, John came up with nifty fakes, little tricks. The puck moved by checks, between legs, and players yelled into the cold, crisp air as they watched it all.

"Hey, John, that's good, how did you do that. You can really handle the puck," Tardiff said afterward.

He put his arm around John for an instant as they headed back towards the house. John's face was flushed, like the rest of the boys'.

"Yeah, I can do that stuff."

As the winter wore on, John became very much a part of the Tardiffs' family life. In many ways, they reminded him of the Ellingboes. His life with the Tardiffs, however, was not without incident.

On one occasion, Poulin brought a kitten home, totally unaware of John's intense dislike for cats and dogs. The pet was a surprise for Martin. John arrived home a short time later and immediately thundered that the feline be

kept away from him. Poulin promised that the cat would
never be allowed to venture into John's upper-story quarters, but the kitten took every opportunity to jump into
John's lap. It became a source of great laughter in the
household, to see the cat's apparent attachment to John,
and the resulting mortified look on John's face.

Poulin enjoyed his camaraderie with John. As a season
ticket holder, he was always in the stands, and often
waited for John outside the dressing room, getting lost in
the throngs of autograph seekers. John was as popular as
any player on the team, and Poulin often got into the act
by pretending to be a security guard, clearing a path
through the fans for the celebrity.

John was always happy to pose for pictures, and was a
willing subject for media and team photographers. One of
the best of these was a picture of Kordic standing next to
Tina Turner after a concert. He became closely acquainted
with Hirsch Billerman, of Billerman Leather Apparel, who
ran newspaper advertisements with John and Nilan featured as models. Bauer skates also produced a poster with
John and Quebec Nordique's Gord Donnelly standing
back-to-back, bare-chested, arms crossed, with menacing
looks on their faces. The ad picked up on the heated rivalry between the two teams, and between the two enforcers, whose bouts were much anticipated by fans and the
media. Their bouts also reflected a battle of wills between
the coaches, who played out a game of one-upmanship
through the fists of their enforcers.

On February 26, 1988, after the posters had been released, John and Donnelly tore into each other at the
opening face-off in the Montreal Forum. Three days later,
they threw down the gloves back in Quebec, not waiting
for the drop of the puck. Both teams were immediately
fined $25,000 each under rule 54(g), which was intro-
duced at the outset of the season as a penalty for fighting
outside the time frame of a period.

The fights were sensationalized, partly because Perron
waded onto the ice in the return match to collar John, and
partly because it was apparent the fights had been planned
as an added measure of hype for the home-and-home series.

In a meeting with NHL vice president Brian O'Neil, Perron was chastised for appearing to condone fighting. Savard privately told Perron the coach could expect a three-game suspension. Perron defended his innocence. He maintained Quebec, as the home team, had posted their lineup first, and had Donnelly penciled in. Before O'Neil, with Savard in attendance, the coach was determined to set the record straight:

"Once and for all, put the responsibility on the players. Stop saying it's always the coaches' fault," Perron stressed during his moment on the carpet.

"I never said to John Kordic you are going to fight this guy. Then all of a sudden, they fight . . . I don't have a walkie-talkie, and I don't have a microphone in his helmet to tell him, 'John, you fight this guy and you fight that guy.' That's not the way it works."

When the sentences were handed down, John and Donnelly were suspended five games each, while Perron and Quebec coach Ron Lapointe were each fined $1,000.

Perron's stability as a coach was already being tested as he attempted a return to the Stanley Cup play-offs—and tried to stick-handle around his players' off-ice behavior.

As the season wound down, the press got wind of another incident and played it up feverishly. This time, the aberration was in the dressing room.

Between periods, Perron had summoned Claude Lemieux to his office, which was adjacent to the dressing room. It was a seemingly routine meeting, with Perron making observations and suggestions about Lemieux's game.

As Lemieux left the coach's office, he exploded in rage, and struck an ashtray so hard, it became dislodged from the bolts that moored it to the wall outside the coach's quarters. The door was still open, and Perron knew the rest of the players were watching.

Perron strode into the dressing room, stopped, and put his hands on his hips: "Claude, what you did, I can't accept it . . . You're not going to play in the third period. Get undressed."

Like John, Lemieux had burst onto the Canadiens scene in the Stanley Cup year. He was a driven player and had a hell-bent knack for pestering and enraging opponents into penalties. He also managed to score 10 goals in the play-offs and emerged, to the surprise of many, as the team's offensive star. He felt he was a proven NHL commodity and was not about to timidly submit to Perron's command.

"You're not going to do that to me," Lemieux shot back. "If there is a performer on your club, it's me . . . I go out and play hard in the shifts all the time . . ."

"Remember that you are not in junior. You are playing professional hockey. You break the lights, you break the ashtray, you break anything that doesn't fit your attitude, but you're not going to do that here," Perron countered.

Lemieux, too far into it, took the confrontation to the next level. He squared off, face-to-face, with Perron. John, who didn't figure in the argument and who wasn't even dressed for the game, grabbed Lemieux from behind, pinning him back, and laid down an option to the irate player of cooling out or regretting a mistake.

Perron, at first perplexed, quickly realized the dynamics and that John's loyalty, despite the complex play of emotions and egos on the team, was unfailingly constant.

Gabby Tardiff began to notice cat toys around the house—little balls with bells inside and furry little dolls. She wondered if the cat was bringing them in from outside.

Late one night, after John had let himself in, and when he was sure everyone was asleep, he turned on a light and pulled a small gift from his pocket. He bent over, letting the cat play with the bow for a moment, then removed the gift wrap which concealed another toy.

Poulin, who had been behind a door, peeking, couldn't resist smiling and entering the room.

"So it was you all along, John," he said.

"What do you mean . . . this, oh, it's nothing."

"C'mon, John, Gabby was thinking the cat was bringing these toys in from outside . . . We never thought it was you . . . So, you like the cat after all, eh, John?"

"Yeah, okay, okay, but just don't tell the players you saw this."

Chapter Fourteen

JEAN PERRON was sitting on a beach in Florida in the summer of 1988 when he found out that the Montreal Canadiens no longer required his services.

Perron seemed to hear or see the damnedest things when he was on vacation, minding his own business. In the summer following the Canadiens' Stanley Cup triumph, Perron was at a table with friends in an Amsterdam bar. Through the din and cigarette smoke, he let his eyes wander for a moment, and noticed a woman at the bar. He did a double take: she seemed familiar, but he couldn't place her. He returned to the conversation, but excused himself a short while later and ambled up to the woman. He told her he knew her from somewhere. She denied ever having met him before, and he returned to his table. Later, in another bar, he noticed the same woman. But this time, he recognized her true identity. The woman was an NHL player dressed in drag. Perron confronted the player, using the man's name. There was silence, a moment of eye contact, and then the player hastily disappeared through the door and into the night. Perron knew he was right, and when he returned to Montreal, he learned the player's secret was a well-known fact among his peers. Clearly, the coach's relationship with his players was somewhat lacking.

• • •

Perron and virtually everyone close to the team knew the success of the season largely depended on the coach's relationship with his players. Perron was not being confided in, nor was his authority respected, if the antics and behavior of players like John, Corson, and Chelios were any indication. Savard had to drop the gavel.

The verdict read like writing on the wall when Pat Burns was announced as the new coach of the Montreal Canadiens.

Burns was one of six children from an Irish father and a French-Canadian mother, and a former junior hockey player who turned down a free-agent tryout with St. Louis in 1969. But it was his 17 years with police forces in Ottawa and Gatineau that leaped off his résumé.

He graduated into the Canadiens organization from junior hockey in the Quebec league. He coached the Hull Olympiques, which took on a patina of instant glamor when Wayne Gretzky purchased the franchise. Among his protégés was future NHL star Luc Robitaille. Burns's tenure with the Olympiques was relatively short—three years—but by then his stock had shot through the roof. His motivational talents and sound interpretations of the game were enough to earn him selection as assistant coach to the Canadian entry in the world junior championships in Czechoslovakia, Christmas 1986.

The following summer, the Canadiens announced that a coaching change would be made in Sherbrooke. Pierre Creamer was leaving the organization to take over the head coaching job in Pittsburgh, where it was thought his French-Canadian background would be an asset in helping to develop Mario Lemieux.

As a hockey town, Sherbrooke was more suited to junior hockey than the AHL. Its fans were as loyal as any, but the annual turnover in an AHL roster meant that the fans had trouble identifying with the players they were paying to watch. Town officials were at loggerheads over the situation with the Winnipeg Jets, which had leased a franchise to the city before the Canadiens. The same argument plagued the relationship with Montreal, which would pull up anchor a year after Burns's departure.

Creamer was big news in the local sports pages and there was strong speculation that his successor would be Jean Hamel, a devoted and deserving assistant coach. Hamel came to the Canadiens presser in Sherbrooke with the same expectation. The anticipation, though, turned to disappointment when Burns strode into the room just before the winning candidate was to be named.

It quickly became understood in Sherbrooke that Burns had zero tolerance for anything but total commitment to the game. On one occasion, for example, after a particularly enervating loss in Sherbrooke, Burns let fly in the dressing room. He roared his disapproval as he crashed around the room, getting right into players' faces. He flung or kicked anything in his path—equipment, sticks, garbage cans. One boot sent a hockey skate whizzing past a player's head. The scene was registered, forever, in the players' memories. They were usually partly or completely undressed, heading to the showers, when Burns unleashed. In the future, several of them reached for their helmets and put them on again until the coach's fury was spent.

Burns was definitely an instrument of change. There was no doubting his convictions, methods, or results. His style was exactly what was needed to restore a sense of order in the dressing room.

Perron alluded to this lack of order in the aftermath of his release as coach of the Montreal Canadiens. He confided, in close circles, that the rogue element on the team had cost him his job.

In the Canadiens' 1988–89 training camp, John was last on the ice, first off, under Burns's watchful eye. His carousing continued, and it cost Kordic big time. The Canadiens decided he wouldn't be joining the team on a preseason road game in Quebec. He was placed on the injury list.

The preseason rolled by and John had not appeared in a

game. He grew desperate, but carried on indulging in his excessive night life. On one occasion, Labonte confronted John about the hockey player's lifestyle. John responded with charm and dismissed his friend's concerns. John continued to train and, when he was satisfied with the results of his weight training, he came to Burns, demanding to play. Their confrontation was intense.

"Burnsy, you gotta get me in there. I'm ready. I want to play."

"John, you're not ready, you know you're not ready, you've gotta work harder in practice, you gotta convince me you're ready."

"Where the fuck you been? I should be playing with Shane, Shane at center and me on the right side. I played with Shane that way all last year."

"John, I was in Sherbrooke, you remember, I don't recall that."

"C'mon, Burnsy, this is bullshit. I'm ready now, right now. What the fuck do I have to do . . . ?"

Burns made it clear that he would never accept any contest of wills, especially one so heavily spiked with vitriol.

Burns eventually put John back into the lineup. John's skill level had slipped so much that he was being considered for the AHL again. There was essentially a single role left for him, his old role as enforcer. Burns hoped it would help bring John back.

In fall 1988, Poulin sensed a change in John. John's behavior was deteriorating even further and he was even more demanding that ever. John was also sniffling a lot, though Poulin pretended not to notice. Instead, he tried to fill John's spare time by surrounding him with family. Martin excelled in his local hockey league and when John could be coaxed, Poulin drove him to the arena to watch the action. In one game, Martin fired a hat trick, and John claimed softly, "I used to do that, score goals, you know." He also discussed with the Tardiffs his growing despair over what appeared to be another year of fighting for a living. He was in the option year of his contract, and the next time he signed, it would be for a quarter-million dollars. He said he was going to buy a $100,000 Ferrari from a friend of a friend. It concerned Poulin that John's money was disappearing faster than he earned it, but he also worried about how John's boasts, his derision with Burns's assignments, and the physical evidence of the resultant on-ice batterings were influencing his son, Martin, who dreamed of becoming an NHL star one day.

John raced down the stairs, and into the kitchen.

"Gabby, you're here, great, I'm late for practice, my Corvette's still in the shop and I need a car."

"John, you know you can use my car. Just ask and I'll give you the keys."

"The Escort . . . Isn't there another car here?"

John's sense of style, his attachment to image, never left him. He made a statement in his Corvette. A Ford Escort, especially a station wagon, was gauche, but he was left with no other choice.

"All right, give me the keys, I gotta go."

John floored the Escort out of the neighborhood. Just before he got to the Forum, he pulled up to a convenience store. He grabbed a newspaper, not looking to see which one, slapped down the change and rushed out the door.

Once inside the car, he rolled down the window slightly and pulled a section of the paper. He neatly tucked a fold of the broadsheet outside the window, keeping the other half inside, and rolled the window back up. The result was good enough—a screen so no one would notice him as he pulled up to the Forum, in a Ford Escort station wagon.

The players were already making their way onto the ice, and Burns saw John running up the hallway to the dressing room. He didn't tolerate late appearances for practice, or excuses.

"Burnsy, they're out there."

"Who's out there?"

"They're out there," John said, pointing to the tall glass partitions from which people inside the Forum could see traffic passing by on St. Catharine street.

"Where, what are you talking about."

Burns followed John up the hallway and out into the lobby near the glass.

"They were there, these guys, they were in a car, they must have gone around the block, the bastards are out there."

Burns peered out, milled around for a moment, then shook his head.

"Well, there's nothing there, get inside and get dressed, we gotta get going."

John labored through the drills, as if he were protesting. He frequently had one of his gloves off and his bare hand up to his nose. He pinched it and wiped it with the back of his hand. Moments later he was at the bench snapping at the trainers to bring him a towel. His nose was bleeding.

"What's the matter, John?" Burns asked.

"Nothin', the air's dry in here."

John pulled up lame part way through the practice. He took a slap shot flush on his skate boot, and the pain was shooting, enough to make him limp.

He was at a point in the day that always felt like hell. He barreled through the gate at the players bench and down the walk to the dressing room.

Burns expected John to resurface in the practice, and when he didn't, he stepped off the ice to peruse the arena and flush out his big winger. Burns found him in the dressing room, naked, but submerged to his upper chest in the bubbling whirlpool. Burns was aware that John carried certain hygienic problems associated with his lifestyle, and didn't belong in the team whirlpool.

"Get the hell outta there, of all the . . . what the hell are you doing . . ."

He had a hockey stick in his hands and his anger was extreme. He swung down hard, leaving dents in the stainless steel tub, and firing salvos at John.

"You better be outta there inside of five seconds or you'll be wearing this thing."

John, beyond embarrassed, barely had time to grab his towel. Retreating to his locker space, he sat down dripping on the cold cement floor, thankful that none of the players were present. He could hear Burns in the background, shouting at the trainers for permitting him to use the whirlpool.

When he exited the Forum, John tore the still-hanging newspaper from the car window. He slammed both hands down onto the steering wheel and clutched it hard. He needed to talk to someone, so he drove to Labonte's apartment.

He barged through the door when Labonte answered it. John paced around the flat and grabbed a bottle of vodka, then plunked it down on the kitchen counter. He slumped into a chair, hung his head in his hands, his eyes gazing down at the table, tears welling, and his fingers holding hair off his forehead.

"Chief, I can't believe what's happening, all this shit. Why are they treating me like this? Why are they doing this to me?"

"Buddy, slow down, talk to me, what are they doing."

"I don't play anymore, it's like everyone thinks I'm this big jerk and I'm not. I want to show them."

"Give it time, man, the people here, they love you, you'll do it and everything will be all right again."

"Oh sure, that's great, but I didn't train all my life to be a fuckin' boxer, I need to play, I train, I'm strong now, so why don't they play me?"

"John, we're friends, right? You got to stop taking that shit, you're doing it all the time and it's fuckin' you up, buddy."

"I don't need your lecture."

"C'mon, John, you used to come down to the gym with me. We used to train good and now you don't come anymore. Did you see yourself with those chicks that time, you were fucked up, man, fucked up. You gotta stop it, man, cause it's gonna stop you."

"What are you, my fuckin' mother?"

John's mood turned to fury. Defiantly, he planted his hands on the table, raised himself, and stormed out the door, not bothering to close it.

It was almost November 1988 and he had appeared in only four games, with no goals and 13 penalty minutes.

Kordic was a powderkeg, inevitably exploding; at times, he truly could not understand what was happening to him or why.

The only tenderness he found outside the Tardiff family was in phone calls back to Edmonton, to Sandy and his family. He loved them. He wanted to marry Sandy, maybe have children. He thought about a big house and lots of kids running around. He knew he could be the person he wanted to be. He also knew it was time to take matters into his own hands. He had to make a stand.

John had strode into Burns's quarters, unannounced. The coach had his head down, reading a paper.

"You wanna turn around and try it all over again?" Burns asked.

"No fuckin' around . . . I've had it with sittin', I wanna play now. I've asked before and I'm tired of sittin' with my thumb up my ass."

"We're not goin' through this again, not with you shooting your mouth off like that. Who do you think I am, some . . ."

Burns didn't have time to finish. John came at him, but stopped at the front of his desk.

"I don't give a fuck anymore, I wanna play now, can you fuckin' hear me?"

His hands were on the desk, and like he had before, he shook it. The front legs lifted off the ground slightly and some papers slid off onto the floor.

John, glaring, made his way to the door. Suddenly, a smashing sound right beside his head. Glass exploding into the wall. Burns had thrown an ashtray at his head.

"You and I'll go out in the alley right now . . . I've been a cop for 17 years, I've been beat up and kicked in the mouth, I've been in more fights than you'll ever see and I don't care. If that's the way you want it then let's go outside right now."

"You're crazy," John said, his voice not quite as hard.

"You got that fuckin' right, I am crazy, and don't you ever fucking forget it."

"You're crazy," John said again, and walked out the door.

News of the confrontation traveled quickly around the

dressing room, but not much farther. Sooner or later, Burns had to take his version up to Savard in the ivory tower, but Savard had already heard enough John stories. His capacity had long since reached overflow, like a barrel left out in the rain too long.

He had floated John's name in trade talk amongst his peers. He could still get good return for big number 31, who still carried the reputation as one of the league's most intimidating enforcers. He had also talked to Toronto Maple Leafs general manager Gord Stellick, and was hoping for a callback, soon.

Chapter Fifteen

IT IS FOUR O'CLOCK in the morning and John Kordic's eyes are wide open. He hears the wind crying outside, like the sounds that fill his nightmares.

Branches scrape against the windowpanes, a rasping sound in his ears. The hardwood floors groan, and all around there are noises in pipes, in the ceiling, from places he can't see.

He curls against the din. The images in his mind torment him. There are images of Sandy there, too, in case he needs them.

He is hot. The sheets are soaked with his sweat. He arches away and wonders what is happening. He realizes he is breathing too fast. There are beads of perspiration at his temples and bugs are crawling under his skin.

His body lashes out from under the covers. The cool air refreshes him for a moment, then he stumbles into the bathroom.

He reaches for a packet, lodged between tissues in a kleenex box. Then he catches a glimpse of his face in the mirror, heavy and red. He is still wearing the sweat-soiled clothes he fell asleep in. He rips off the shirt, the jeans, the socks.

The packet now, in his hands. He is familiar with its contents. He has a terrible longing for that feeling again . . .

Afterwards, he flips the switch and the light dies. It

leaves white shadows in his eyes. Only out the window is there any light. He uses it as a guide back to his bed.

Outside, the sound of a car, and its light breaching his window and traveling across the wall. He believes they are watching him, driving by his window and watching. He springs up to the window, but stands away from it by the curtain. He sees the car disappear, but doesn't believe it's really gone. They're there.

He spends a half hour by the window, biting his fingernails, hiding behind the curtain, peering out.

"They're coming to get me," he says aloud.

Down now, down the stairs, past calls from Gabby and Poulin. The need to hide from them. He can do it outside, rage against them.

He bounds from one bush to another, low to the ground. When the wind blows, he yells out his conviction again, "They're coming to get me!"

Back inside, still in his underwear. He is by the phone. He needs to talk to Sandy. Gabby and Poulin are there. He tells them he needs to talk to Sandy. Gabby dials a number, keeping the key pad from John's view. She speaks in a low tone for a few moments, then hangs up.

A short while later, a car comes, and it turns into the driveway. Burns and assistant general manager Andre Bourdrea get out and knock on the door.

All his experiences with people had furnished Burns with an ability to judge human behavior. He was barely three months into his job when he faced his first test of wills with his players. He had made the rounds to all the regular player hangouts—Chez Paree, the nightclub called Thursdays—talking to doormen, trying to come off as a nice guy. He'd ask if they had seen any of his guys inside. Most of them knew who he was and cooperated. The players, though, decided the coach wasn't going to trespass into every corner of their territory; they designated a bar on St. Laurent Street, and convinced the staff to keep the premises off-limits to Burns. When he came calling, Burns was told the bar was full. He accepted the explanation at first, then realized he was marked as the bear in the apiary. He returned, demonstrating that he was not an undesirable person, that he simply wanted to sit down and have a beer. Eventually, the manager came to the door: we don't want any problems, Mr. Burns, we don't need this kind of problem, he said. When Burns returned, the bouncers hastened to open doors for him, and show him a table. Let this guy in anytime, they told their colleagues. During practice, the next day, he called his players together. They huddled around him on the ice. They were expecting his regular address.

"I found your hangout, I talked to the owner, and I'm a full-fledged member," he said as heads bowed. "Nice try."

Now, there was only room for compassion. It would have been a peculiar sight to the press. They had chronicled his every coaching move—and made much of his fiery manner. When his anger peaked, cameramen zoomed in for a closeup, playing it into thousands of living rooms across the nation. He was also questioned every time he sat a French-Canadian player. It was between those vicissitudes that he came to John.

Burns convinced John to come back to the Forum to talk things through. Poulin followed in his car. John was mostly silent. He walked with the coach into his office.

"John, you wanna tell me what's wrong?"

"I want to play, I want to help the team."

"John, before you do that, you have to get yourself right. If you're not 100 percent, you're not going to help anyone. You've got to get back to being John Kordic. You're not going to practice for now."

"But I want to practice, come on . . ."

"No, you'll only end up making things worse for yourself. I want you to go home and think about it, John."

Burns watched John leave the office. He knew Poulin would put John into his car and take care of him.

In a few hours, he would have to talk to Savard. There was an ultimatum concerning John, and they were both aware of it. John had only a few hours left as a Montreal Canadiens player.

Burns left the Forum alone. Outside, the sun was already up on a new day.

Chapter Sixteen

ON MONDAY November 8, 1988, Gord Stellick and Serge Savard agreed to terms on a trade that would send Russ Courtnall to Montreal in exchange for John and a sixth-round draft choice.

John knew his days had long been numbered in Montreal. He sat around after practices chatting up those in the media who still cared to listen to him. He no longer measured his words. Anyone close to the team had also accurately calculated John's fate. John's bitterness was apparent when he told the press that he did not train to become a boxer.

Savard delivered the word to John. It was a brief conversation. The sordid details of John's behavior had so eroded their four-year relationship that all the two could manage with civility were a few words to each other. The media was offered the same brevity. Savard spoke with reserve on the subject of John's career. When pressed for details about their relationship he insisted that it was too personal to be conveyed to the public. If there was a widely believed reason for the trade, it was that John's incessant complaints over ice time had sealed his fate.

Certainly, Savard could never publicly decry John's problems without the risk of sentencing the hockey player to an automatic life suspension under the NHL's zero-tolerance drug policy. The policy left it to member clubs to independently rehabilitate their players, should the need arise. The league was effectively absolved of such duties. It could only intervene in the event of an arrest.

Savard never released a single detail on whether or not the Canadiens ever sought medical help for John. Consequently, it was widely believed by the press, by Labonte, and by many Canadiens players who were close to John, that Savard ultimately decided to trade John rather than get treatment for him. When the trade was eventually made, Stellick, like the media, was kept in the dark.

When the deal was announced, Savard received kudos as a master of making effective trades. During his four-year tenure as general manager, most of his trades had been described in flattering terms. He had swapped Lemieux for Sylvain Turgeon, Rick Wamsley for St. Louis first- and second-round draft picks, which turned out to be Corson and Richer. In trading John, Savard's reputation received further critical acclaim.

Stellick welcomed John to the Toronto Maple Leafs over the phone. At age 30, the NHL's youngest executive, he wanted to demonstrate a touch of class and speak to his newest player, even though the opportunity to meet in person would come the next day.

Stellick was impressed with John, and surprised by his candidness. During his negotiations with Savard, Stellick had learned that the Edmonton Oilers had shown interest in John. Had the Leafs not completed the deal on Monday, Savard would have turned his full attention to Edmonton's proposal. John was taken aback when he learned he was going to Toronto. He had confided to Labonte, his other friends, and some members of the press that he was about to become an Oiler. He was dismayed at first. But he also anticipated a return to a role as a regular contributor.

Stellick lost sleep anticipating the reaction to his latest trade. He had come a long way since his days writing out lineup cards for Leafs owner Harold Ballard in 1975. He never believed he was being groomed for the general manager's position; Ballard was not one to wax eloquent about promotions. But his career hopes suddenly improved in

February 1988 when Ballard ended a miserable note in the team's managerial history and fired Gerry McNamara.

When the nineties began, Harold Ballard entered the final chapter of his life. His character was as forceful as ever, but his health was rapidly deteriorating. By 1988, all the major daily newspapers in Toronto had lengthy obituaries at the ready in the event of Ballard's sudden passing. Much of what Ballard touched was affected by the state of his health, especially the value of Maple Leaf Gardens stock. As long as he was alive, there was an aura around the Gardens, although for most of the public and the media it had the taint of a soap opera. Ballard's final years could not have been happy ones. His team was suffering, almost moribund from years of losing, and his family had aligned themselves against one another to secure a share of the old man's incredible estate.

When the Leafs needed a definitive hand to guide them out of their woeful slump, Ballard appointed a triumvirate to manage the team for the remainder of the 1987–88 season. Stellick thereby entered a peculiar relationship with head coach John Brophy and director of scouting Dick Duff to run the team.

Brophy had long harbored the belief that as head coach he had been compromised by the lack of size and toughness on his team. This was a thorn in his side, one he complained about at management meetings.

Up to that point, Stellick's rapport with Brophy had been excellent. And he tried to maintain it by demonstrating concern for Brophy's concerns. The first player move the triumvirate made was the acquisition of Brian Curran, a veteran defenseman with frequent fighting points, from the New York Islanders for a sixth-round draft choice.

As an organization, the Leafs remained mired in gloom after an exit from a first-round play-off meeting with Detroit. To make matters worse, Ballard had left the general manager position empty for too long, and was forced to resolve the situation before the NHL draft in June 1988.

Like Stellick, Ballard enjoyed Brophy's company. He enjoyed the ragged edge of Brophy's experience as a player in the East Coast league, and the yarns from those halcyon days. He identified with the school of hard knocks Brophy came from. Brophy, whose straight white hair contrasted with his hard features and the seasoned look of a barroom brawler, seemed to boil red in moments of anger. He swore readily, and in a way that made those who knew him laugh. Ballard referred to him as "his kind of man," and while Brophy was coach, Ballard furnished him with a new Oldsmobile every three months and had his suits perfectly pressed and hung in his Gardens locker. Ballard toyed with the idea of handing Brophy a dual portfolio of head coach and general manager, but instead named Stellick as general manager in April.

Brophy had undermined his chances as general manager just before the play-offs when he attempted to have Borje Salming removed from the team. Salming, like Courtnall, Miroslav Frycer, and several other players, found himself lodged in Brophy's doghouse. Their crimes were largely circumstantial; they were finesse players who failed to show the grit Brophy demanded. With Salming, though, Brophy was walking on thin ice. The elegant Swede was among Ballard's all-time favorite players. Ballard often sat high in the red section, watching Salming skate in practices and marveling at the player's talents. Brophy's anti-Salming crusade earned him a lecture from Ballard, and did nothing to advance his chances of becoming general manager.

Stellick approached the draft with as much diplomacy as possible. His intentions were to strengthen his alliance with Brophy. Shortly after he was rebuked by Ballard, Brophy phoned Stellick and declared he would lend his full cooperation to a smooth draft.

Stellick walked through a mine field to arrive at a game plan for the draft. Much of the public's impression with Brophy was still favorable. During the play-offs, fans, many of them teenage girls, scooped up replica top hats which had the words "Brophy's Boys" stenciled in a gold stipple across the brim. During the play-off run, though, the public was afforded a rare glimpse into the dressing room, which changed the public's attitude toward Brophy. With four games remaining in the regular season, Leaf enforcer Dave Semenko woke up early one morning, packed his bags, and left the team. Roommate Greg Terrion was the only person he informed about his plans. When reporters finally caught up with him, he said that his personal anguish had simply stolen the fun from the game. The press speculated that Brophy drove Semenko towards emotional breakdown by keeping him on a short leash on the bench, turning him loose to fight, then putting him back on the bench again until a similar situation arose.

When the Leafs' brief flirtation with the postseason ended, Frycer cut into Brophy. He told the press that the mood in the dressing room was cancerous, that at least 90 percent of the players refused to play committed for Brophy. A quote from an anonymous player concurs with Frycer's analysis: "He ripped the hearts out of every guy on this team, one by one." Many players and fans also believed Brophy made a colossal tactical error when he insulted Red Wings coach Jacques Demers by feigning the choke sign. The Leafs had a 3–1 lead in games at the time, but the Wings came back to clinch the series. It was as apparent to Stellick as it was to most Leaf observers that Brophy's coaching legs were collapsing under him.

Even with the smell of decay pervading the Leafs' dressing room, Ballard could not tie a can to Brophy so soon after McNamara's dismissal. The appearance of instability, to his players, the public, and the rest of the league, would be too damaging. Instead, Ballard publicly endorsed Brophy as the best coach in the NHL.

When the draft rolled around, Stellick announced the Leafs would be selecting Scott Pearson, a tough and physical winger from Bill LaForge's Niagara Falls Thunder. That left Martin Gelinas, who would prove to be a much more prudent choice, still in the selection pool. In the second round, the Leafs chose Tie Domi, the OHL's penalty king who already had a huge following. It was a case of being in the right place at the right time for Domi, who was pegged by NHL central scouting as a middle- to late-round selection at best. At the end of the first round, Brophy leaned over to Stellick at the draft table with an eleventh hour pitch to land Link Gaetz. The request never got out of the starting gate.

The Leafs new players were a public-relations success. It had been much the same with Luke Richardson, the Leafs' first-round pick the previous year. Scouting director Floyd Smith underlined Joe Sakic as the team's top objective, but Brophy stressed that he couldn't stomach another small centerman.

The Leafs made believers out of their followers at the outset of the 1988–89 season with an 8–3–1 run in their first 12 games. Courtnall remained in Brophy's doghouse, leaving Danny Daoust as the team's fourth center, behind Ed Olczyk, Vincent Damphousse, and Tom Fergus.

The Leafs lost a Halloween game to St. Louis, right before they were to return home to the Gardens for a first-place overall showdown with the Boston Bruins. Brophy re-opened his bid to have Domi in the lineup for the game. His concern over the level of toughness on his team was undying. By the time the Bruins rolled into town, his concerns were legitimate.

Stellick insisted that even if Domi was summoned from the Peterborough Petes, he was not ready for prime time, and would quickly be dispatched to junior. Stellick, though, could not overlook his team's obvious lack of toughness. Wendel Clark, the Leafs' leading physical presence, was rocked with injuries that were to keep him sidelined for 65 games. Chris McRae, with the AHL Newmarket Saints, was the only other apparent tough guy in the franchise. Team scouts, however, rated him a step below the level of preparation needed to join the NHL team.

The Bruins handed the Leafs another loss. Brophy shuffled his lineup, aligning as much toughness as he could from the available manpower. His tamperings left Stellick, most players, and the press both derisive and desperate for another win. The rest of the NHL took note, and when the Leafs played Los Angeles on November 6, 1988, it was like a punch in the face.

The Kings skated all over the listless Leafs. When they had built up a lead, Kings enforcer Marty McSorley ran Salming heavily into the boards. There was no one to answer the infraction, even mildly. McSorley continued to wreak havoc with Salming and other Leafs. He had a free hand to scuttle them all night, and he knew it. At face-offs near the Leafs' bench, he fired challenges and insults at the players. Again, no one stepped forward to stand up for the Maple Leafs, and all the while, Brophy was doing a slow burn.

Brophy was back in Stellick's office the next day, still smarting with embarrassment. He mentioned John's name for the first time. When Brophy was coach of the Canadiens' AHL Halifax affiliate, he'd known John. He had noticed John wasn't playing under Pat Burns, and floated the idea that it would be an opportune time to inquire about his availability.

Stellick began his own reconnaissance work on John. He had been weathering the losing skid and appeasing Courtnall's discontent, who came to his office every other day wondering when he would be playing again. At the time, the Leafs' resources did not leave Stellick with many avenues of inquiry into John's background. The team's scouting system was one of the weakest in the NHL. Stellick had never heard a word about John's drug dependency. He had heard rumors that John was a loose cannon, a hard partyer, a handful in the way that Bob Probert, Behn Wilson, and a long list of others were a handful.

On the Friday before the trade, Stellick phoned Savard and floated the offer for Courtnall. Savard phoned back Saturday, eager to discuss and to close, Courtnall being the best offer for John by far. Stellick said he wanted one more day to weigh the situation. He spoke with Brophy, who by now was extremely excited and anxious about completing the trade. Stellick ran the trade by Ballard, and was surprised by his boss's ready acceptance. Ballard liked Courtnall as a player, but he also felt a trade would have a positive impact on his team's faltering situation. He gave Stellick his blessing. Stellick turned for advice to assistant coach Garry Larivierre. Larivierre said Stellick would be passing up the opportunity of making executive of the year if he didn't make the trade.

Stellick's grab bag of opinions was enough to convince him to make the trade. He was also aware of his team's overwhelming lack of physical presence; when Brophy had mentioned John's name, Stellick had recognized a possible solution to their problems. He thought about his own performance as a general manager. He thought about the Stanley Cup, "the promised land," he called it. It was a wonderful thought, and as much as he liked Brophy and wanted to have a good relationship with him, he questioned whether Brophy was the coach to take the Leafs to the promised land. He decided that Brophy was not going to deliver a championship. At the same time, he had seen McNamara manipulate Ballard and pave an exit for other Leaf coaches. The phrase "greasing the skids" ran through his mind, and he decided he wouldn't play the game that way.

On Monday, he got Savard to throw in a sixth-round pick and agreed to the trade. He was going to give his coach the one player he thought the entire organization really wanted.

Chapter Seventeen

JOHN DIALED Poulin's number from a pay phone in the Forum. He had a list of things to do before his flight to Toronto, and he asked for Martin to pick him up.

Just before Martin arrived, he went into the Forum's sport shop. On a rack of NHL sweaters, he spotted a Maple Leafs team jersey. It made him feel good to see the store still stocked with plenty of Canadiens' No. 31 Kordic jerseys. He plucked a Leaf jersey and had his name sewn onto the back.

When Martin came, he posed for a picture, and signed it later as a gift to the Tardiff family. The press also got hold of it, and ran the picture on the sports sections the following day.

When John walked into the Gardens later in the day, several Leafs players were in the dressing room.

"Hi, John Kordic here, I just got in from Montreal, how's it goin'."

The players turned for a moment. They had been riveted by a televised broadcast of a boxing match. They were glad to finally meet John, and were immediately struck by the fact that he was much larger in person than they thought.

John sat beside Chris Kotsopoulos, the Leafs' burly defenseman. He reached to shake his hand.

"Hey, what kind of endorsements can you get here?" John asked.

"Come again . . ."

"You know, what kind of endorsements, do you guys do that kind of stuff?"

"Yeah right, I don't know where you're coming from, but this is Toronto, that stuff don't exist."

It wasn't Kotsopoulos's intention to underscore John's naïveté. He was merely being truthful. The Leafs, ten years departed from the wonderful 1978 campaign and Lanny McDonald's overtime goal that beat the mighty New York Islanders, were the brunt of jokes with the fans and media. While the fans' love affair with hockey meant capacity audiences at the Gardens, the Leafs themselves were hardly marketable commodities.

John was also in for a further disappointment.

"Where do you guys park for practices here?" he asked Kotsopoulos.

"Did you pay to park now?"

"Yeah."

"You get a paycheck, right?"

"Yeah."

"Good, join the club. We all pay for parking around here. Sit down and enjoy the fight."

John's introduction to his second NHL team was more a reality adjustment than a continuation of the success he had enjoyed thus far. He was 23 years old, paid more than $7,000 every two weeks, and had all three of hockey's major championships under his belt. Hockey fans in Montreal had placed him on a pedestal reserved for the game's premiere stars. Although he'd scored only seven goals in his three seasons with the Montreal Canadiens, there had been constant recognition in the streets, swarms of autograph seekers, and always his name ringing in the stands: *Kordic! Kordic! Kordic!* He arrived in Toronto to heaps of news copy, most of it critical: the Leafs exchanged a skilled player for a goon—the word he most hated. He'd found out from other players that there would be few endorsements, that the Leafs were not marketable commodities. Moreover, the team lacked adequate weight-lifting and training equipment. He found an ally in Brophy, and cordial greetings from Stellick and Ballard. Beyond that, he was left in the Westbury Hotel with a very short time in which to find an apartment.

As well as being charmed by Johns's wit and candor, Stellick was impressed by John's bulk. Stellick remembered one of the most classic fights he ever witnessed, a bout between John and Wendel Clark at the Forum in January 1988. The two had earmarked each other for scraps in John's final year in Portland, when Clark was with the Saskatoon Blades. Those fights were rated as even, and when they renewed their hostilities at the Forum, Wendel landed several blows most observers thought were damaging. Suddenly, though, John cracked a roundhouse left off Wendel's head, and wobbled him noticeably. The linesman stepped in immediately. Many believe that Clark's recurring hand injury was a result of that fight. John gave him an exaggerated wink and skated off to the penalty box.

Stellick also recalled Brophy's claims that John was instrumental in the Canadiens' Stanley Cup win. But he began to wonder about that perception, especially when John told him that he'd spent a large portion of his spare time at that time in limousines with big-breasted girls from wet-T-shirt contests.

John worked out regularly in the dressing room's weight-training facility. He also dropped to the floor after every game and practice, and beat out 100 pushups with his hands together.

After John's first few games, Brophy realized that he was seeing a different player from the one he coached against in the AHL. While John's strength was unquestionable, his level of aerobic fitness was poor. There were obvious signs—labored breathing, sweating, especially from the temples, and marginal stamina. Brophy passed his observations on to Stellick, who was only beginning to piece together the puzzle that was his latest acquisition.

John rented an apartment near the Gardens, without a roommate. Although within steps of the night life, he was alone most nights during the home portion of the Leafs' schedule. He was also a short walk from a stretch of Jarvis Street that ran through the heart of the Track, a police euphemism for a blight on the map of Toronto where sex was for sale, and along with it, drugs, pornography—anything.

By December 1988, the buoyancy of the season-opening success dissipated as Leafs losses piled up. During a game in Pittsburgh, Brophy, who left little doubt about the parameters of John's assignments, sent him onto the ice with less than a minute remaining in another defeat. John promptly got his stick into an opponent's face, triggering a brawl and a misconduct.

As soon as the team was back at the Gardens, Stellick rang down to the coach's office. He would not tolerate such an infraction, but he didn't blame John. Rather, he questioned Brophy's rationale in sending John out so late in the game, obviously with one purpose in mind. It made the whole organization look like a sideshow.

Several days later, on December 10, John charged after Keith Acton, brought his stick over Acton's head, and jerked it backward, breaking Acton's nose. John received only a minor penalty on the play. In effect, though, it was a lightning rod, seen on national television, a blatant example of what critics claimed should be eradicated from the game.

In private, John blamed the incident on Brophy, who challenged Kordic's manhood in verbal thrashings between periods. The play was included in one of Don Cherry's popular "Rock 'em, Sock 'em" videos, primarily because of the running commentary on the play-by-play, which stated, "You have to be from the acorn family to come up with a move like that." The Leafs absorbed further critical bashing in the media. John would have his day before NHL executive vice president Brian O'Neil, who summoned him to Montreal.

John flew to Montreal with Stellick, and told his general manager that he felt like a school kid being called down to the principal's office. When John entered O'Neils office, O'Neil asked him for an explanation. John said he was merely trying to hook Acton and hold him back. He didn't mean to break his nose, he told O'Neil.

Two days later, O'Neil handed John a ten-game suspension, without pay. John was furious. Part of his anger was over the loss of wages. Stellick tried to appease John by figuring the deduction into John's overall pay schedule. He challenged John to use the layoff constructively to work himself back into shape. John's fitness level was still below an acceptable standard. He was sniffling a lot and frequently complained he was fighting a cold.

With time on his hands, John would venture out to Church Street, and head to a sandwich shop on Yonge near Carleton, a block away from the Gardens. John, in tight jeans and a leather jacket, became a common sight at that location. John never knew he was being watched.

The Westbury Hotel was also one of John's favorite haunts. One night in December 1988, he sat at the bar nursing a beer, then moved to a booth. There he met with two Lebanese men, brothers, who he knew from Edmonton. They had arranged to meet. The brothers operated an "escort service" stocked with beautiful women. In the past, they had visited Montreal to see John, who they valued as one of their best customers. John, who had earnest feelings for one of the women at their service, would give them handfuls of money, especially if they brought along cocaine, which he considered an aphrodisiac. When he was in Edmonton, he would also give them the keys to his Corvette, which they would drive around so that Sandy wouldn't notice it parked at a hotel.

John also became buddies with a rock musician who played around Toronto. Known as "Magic," he was handsome, with long hair gelled and combed straight back, in what John referred to as the "Gino look." Magic also ran a limousine service during the day. Limousines had become one of John's favorite modes of transportation, and he rented them exclusively from Magic. He referred to them as his office. In Montreal, John had enjoyed the ostentation of pulling up to nightclubs in a limo. Whenever Sandy visited him, he would send a stretch to the airport and have it rendezvous with him outside the Gardens main doors after practice. If he had other commitments when she arrived, he would hand Sandy several hundred-dollar bills, tuck her back into the limo, and tell her to go shopping until he could see her later.

By Christmas 1988, Sandy had become a significant part of John's life. He flew to Edmonton over the NHL's Christmas break to be with her. He had been staying at Sandy's apartment for increasingly longer periods of time in the off-season. Since meeting her in the summer after the Canadiens' Stanley Cup triumph, he had racked up hundreds of dollars in long-distance bills. He phoned her almost every night, and wrote to her every day. His love letters were corny, hopelessly romantic, sexy. He sometimes drew a caricature of her tiny pet dog at the bottom of the page, next to his name.

On Christmas Day, he hauled in a large box which he spent over an hour wrapping. It was topped with a huge bow, and he set it before the Christmas tree.

Sandy's mother, Noreen, giggled as John pretended he could barely lift the box, that it might tear through the floor if he set it down. Sandy knew what the box contained—a tiny velvet case cradling an engagement ring. She smiled and looked into John's eyes. She had grown to love his wonderful playfulness. For over a year, however, she had imagined a different scene: a hazy moment of romance and spontaneity. When the moment arrived, in her mother's apartment, she couldn't tell John the oversize box didn't measure up to her expectations. Instead, she played along, pulling out the reams of shredded white paper, until she found the velvet box nestled at the bottom.

On Boxing Day, John told her he wanted to spend the last night of the break alone with her. He was dressed smartly when he arrived in his Corvette, and they headed off to the Fantasy Island Hotel near the West Edmonton Mall, and to the suite John had reserved. John brought out a chair and placed it in the middle of the main room. He asked her to sit in it. There was soft music on the stereo, and he was behind her, telling her to relax and be still. Then he wrapped a satiny blindfold around her head. John handed her a bouquet of roses, and asked her to count them. She counted eleven roses. She wondered where the twelfth one was, and what he was up to. He asked her to remove the blindfold, and when she opened her eyes, he was holding the twelfth rose, with the engagement ring around the stem. Her dream was realized, and she was swept away. All of John's problems and struggles seemed so very far away.

John returned to Toronto to learn that rumors of Brophy's demise as coach of the Toronto Maple Leafs were grounded in fact.

On December 23, 1988, Stellick had phoned down to the coach's office and asked Brophy to meet him in the second-floor executive quarters. Brophy took the walk, as if he were being summoned to the gallows, knowing it was Ballard who had given the nod to Stellick to carry out the dirty work. The actual delivery was simple, "We're going to make a coaching change."

As the ship's master and captain, Ballard asked to see Brophy one final time. He was in the quiet of his own Gardens apartment, where no camera or tape recorder had ever been allowed. Ballard said he wished things were different and offered Brophy the opportunity to stay on as a scout. Brophy declined the offer.

There could be no denying how Ballard felt about his coach. When Brophy unlocked the door to the coach's room each morning, he would often find Ballard there, in his boxer shorts, shaving, clanking his razor into the sink. "Your team was horseshit last night," the old man would say, his face contorting around the razor strokes. Ballard enjoyed Brophy in his element. When he came to the Leafs, Brophy was a hockey legend despite his undistinguished career. Brophy was said to be the inspiration behind the 1977 hockey movie *Slapshot,* which starred Paul Newman. Brophy was Ogie Ogglethorp. He punished opponents, made them spit their teeth out. Once, an angry fan fired a gun at him through a window vent while he was in a shower. When Brophy was asked by *Toronto Sun* columnist Scotty Morrison why he had never seen the movie, he replied, "Why the hell would I watch it, I lived it."

Brophy, who left Toronto almost immediately afterward, went on to become coach of the Hampton Road

Admirals of the East Coast Hockey League, his old alma mater.

Ballard entrusted the coaching duties for the remainder of the season to George Armstrong, who reluctantly stepped forward from his scouting duties. As coach, Armstrong relied heavily on assistant coach Garry Larivierre, a former NHL player. Larivierre had been quietly assigned to supervise John. He attempted to form a friendship with John, and on road trips, often bunked in the hotel room adjacent to him.

In the new year, Stellick summoned John to his office after he was contacted by a Metro Toronto police officer about the hockey player's activities. Undercover officers from the morality squad were trying to rid the Track of prostitutes and the accompanying drug trade. They had noticed a tall man in jeans and a leather jacket walking around the area under surveillance. He was conspicuous, an outsider. Being hockey fans, they had soon recognized him. One evening they arrested a prostitute from New York who had been with John. During their interrogation of the woman, they uncovered sordid details about Kordic. She said drugs were involved, but throughout their observations, they never witnessed John actually make a buy.

When Stellick confronted John, the hockey player denied the allegations, claiming that he was trying to make friends in a new city. Word of the allegations, and of the police tip, soon made its way into the dressing room. Stellick warned John to stay away from this element, for himself and for the team.

Rumors were already circulating about John, the way they had in Montreal. Players began hearing about the Westbury Hotel, about his antics on the road. They also saw the rented limousines, at the airport, after practices and games. They saw the characters John called friends, witnessed his sniffling and constant cold symptoms. All of it only served to erode the respect his fellow players had for him.

On road trips, when the team wasn't playing the next day and had a later flight out of town, the players would often hold impromptu parties. Sometimes they had the entire floor of the hotel rented out, and would wander from room to room, towels wrapped around their waists and beers in hand. John rabble-roused with the best of them. Initially, he paid little mind to references of "Sniffy," a nickname prefixed to his name. Since Portland, he had learned to ignore this kind of needling. In the dressing room, though, he took exception to remarks from Dan Daoust, and exploded into a bitter fight. The media dutifully recorded the incident, giving it mild acknowledgment in the day's Leafs coverage.

The press wasn't on hand, though, for another dressing-room incident in which John is alleged to have thrashed Gary Leeman. John was closely allied to Al Iafrate, whose own wild side and emotional flare-ups are well-documented. Part of Iafrate's problems began with his wife, Missy, who was rumored to be having an affair with Leeman. Occasionally, those players who were married went out together on couples-only evenings, and Missy was often seen at one end of a table with Leeman, while Al was absorbed in a conversation at the opposite end. Behind closed doors, John apparently hammered revenge into Leeman. Other players, who didn't witness the incident, began hearing that Al Secord had delivered Leeman's comeuppance. When the press finally caught up, the incident became the talk of the town. Virtually every player, on record, maintained the entire affair was a fabrication. The press, in turn, treated it as a hot and juicy rumor, breaking the players' code of silence. Leeman was dogged by the incident from inside and outside the dressing room. The players closed ranks, protecting Leeman from further character assassination. They understood how to handle the press, were schooled in cliché responses.

During the height of the Leeman controversy, the Leafs returned home from a road trip to Chicago. They touched down at Pearson International Airport, into a brutal sub-zero cold snap and snowfall. The players discovered that the harsh conditions had killed the battery power in their cars. As they scrambled for taxis and jumper cables, John sauntered into a waiting limo. As the car circled to leave, John noticed Leeman was among the unfortunate, victimized by the weather. Leeman appeared to venture closer to the limo, as if to inquire about a boost. John calmly rolled the window down and with a smirk said, "See ya later, scumbag."

The season wound down to a disappointing finale. On the last game of the year, the team's tenuous play-off hopes were scuttled on Todd Gill's giveaway against Chicago, an infamous footnote he didn't deserve.

John had been used sparingly by Armstrong, and not at all in the season's closing games. During one game against the Canadiens, when he was stranded on the bench, there were dozens of Kordic jerseys in the seats at the Forum. Dejected, John bolted to the dressing room at the final buzzer while his mates skated down for the traditional show of support for the goalie. Stellick took Armstrong aside afterward, explaining that John had deserved at least one shift that game.

On the plane ride back to Toronto, the flight attendants were kept busy bringing John and the rest of the players drinks.

Partway through the flight, John rocketed out of his seat towards the front where the coaches were sitting.

"Hey, Bimmer, how do ya think it fuckin' feels, sittin' on the end of the bench." He had put away several drinks, and now he hovered over Larivierre, his hands clutching the edges of the assistant coach's seat.

Chicago had dispatched enforcer Wayne Van Dorp on the ice, and he'd run Leeman hard into the boards several times. The Hawks were trailing at the time, but stormed back to tie and eventually win the game. Stellick recalled later that Van Dorp's targeting of Leeman was a factor in the changing tides in the game. John never got the chance to take to the ice to protect Leeman—of all things,.

"Van Dorp got to play and I didn't get one shift."

"John, it's like I told you, you know you add 20 pounds to every man on the team just by being on the bench . . ."

"Yeah, well, all I know is Van Dorp got to play, he got a shift in the third period and I get squat, how's that, how do ya think it feels?"

Larivierre wanted to say more, but John wouldn't let him. The assistant coach was shaking. Stellick looked on, shocked and stunned, as did Armstrong. They all looked at one another, at John. They all swallowed hard for a nervous moment.

John returned to his seat, flustered, and picked up his drink.

Before the plane landed, he got hold of the flight attendant's microphone.

"This is Johnny K, just wanna wish you guys a good season. I was the guy sitting with his thumb up his ass all night."

John elicited some laughter from the players. Since he had an audience, he took aim at several players and incidents in a rollicking stand-up comedy routine.

"Hey, Giller."

Gill turned in his seat.

"I just got to ask you one question . . ."

"Yeah, what's that?"

"What the fuck were you thinking on that play?"

In a moment that could have ruined the evening, the players decided instead to laugh. They laughed hard at John—and with him.

"Marshy."

"Yes, John," Brad Marsh replied innocently.

"Question . . . what's your favorite football team in the NFL?"

Marsh pondered for a moment, then came the punch line: "The Cleveland Browns . . ."

John stressed the Browns part, and again the plane filled with laughter.

He wished everyone a good off-season, and wrapped up with "I love you guys."

John was happy if he felt his teammates accepted him for who he was. It was the boyish innocence in him, the element of his character that made him likable. Two days after the season ended, John lost that last piece of his innocence. He flew home to Edmonton, to the most devastating news he would ever hear. He learned that his father had been diagnosed with cancer. Ivan had only months to live.

Chapter Eighteen

WHEN THE TIME came, John was not prepared for his father's death. After he died, Ivan was factored into the growing number of stories that focused on John's problems on and off the ice. Virtually all these analyses related John's difficulties to his apparent inability to make his father happy. Very few people, however, including members of the media, understood the complexity of that problem. John may have done his best to please his father, but Ivan simply wanted more for his son. He'd proudly watched his son develop into one of the best defensemen in Edmonton minor hockey, then a WHL all-star and finally a player in the NHL. When John developed into an enforcer, however, Ivan was disturbed. Players were out there to play, not to fight. His son's welfare meant more to him than the game of hockey, or the men who ran it. When John slipped towards drug dependency, Ivan had to appeal to those same men to help him get his son back on track. For Ivan, a source of great joy was gradually transformed into one of grave concern.

John had tried to explain to Ivan and to Regina that fighting had become part of his job description. Ivan steadfastly refused to give his blessing to this behavior. Although John became resigned to his father's disappointment, he was never resigned to his not making Ivan proud. John also felt he'd let his father down in his personal life. Ivan did not think that Sandy was a suitable mate for John, and let him know it, calling her "skunky" because she sometimes dyed blond streaks into her hair.

Each hockey season, John had to decide whether he should listen to his father, or his coaches; ultimately, he obeyed the latter. Each fight placed him farther away from his father. By the time Ivan became ill, it was too late for the two to resolve the complex set of issues separating them.

John remained by his father's side for much of the summer, then left in September to join the Leafs in training camp. The organization's sympathy was with him, as was its respect for the character he showed in following through with his professional obligation.

Sandy drove John's Corvette to Toronto, and parked it at the Westbury Hotel. When she found John, she hugged him. John drove off for a while, saying he had to attend to some business. Shortly after he returned, the phone rang in his room. Sandy answered it, and without a word, handed the receiver to John. It was a call from Edmonton. John put down the receiver, and stared at the bed. He curled his lower lip under his front teeth, clearly trying to control himself, but it was no use. Sobs overwhelmed him.

"I can't believe he's really gone," he said.

Hours after Ivan died, the Leafs absorbed an unpopular 7–1 loss against the Buffalo Sabres in their home opener.

Boos rained down from the seats. New coach Doug Carpenter ignored the taunts and jeers that were urging him to get back to his former coaching post in New Jersey. John sat alone on the end of the bench after the final whistle blew. Voices from the seats rained down on him as well. He was called a bum.

Sandy sat by John's bed for most of the night. In the morning, they flew back to Edmonton.

The Leafs gave John as much time as was necessary to grieve. At one point, while he was still in Edmonton after Ivan's death, John disappeared. No one knew where he went, and though some friends asked, they never found out the truth. He was just gone.

PART TWO

"This guy is going to die."

Chapter Nineteen

MARIO MAURO drove a Porsche 928 and lived in a posh semi in the Yonge Street and Lawrence Avenue area of Toronto. These symbols of luxury never sat well with his fellow police officers, who earned the same wages as Mauro but who couldn't afford flashy cars or upscale neighborhoods.

Mauro, 35, sometimes moonlighted as a real-estate agent and had a family land-development business waiting in the wings. Coupled with the innuendo and rumor surrounding him, these were sufficient reasons, in his opinion, to support a career change. After seven years of service, Mauro retired from the force.

John met Mauro at P.M. Toronto, a nightclub close to the Gardens, which provided an exclusive party lounge for the Leafs. John loved Mauro's car. He also thought Mario looked like Cheech, of Cheech and Chong fame. Mauro, who John took to calling Cheech, agreed to put Kordic up in a room at his home: an arrangement that was viewed suspiciously by the boys in the morality squad.

By this time, in the fall of 1989, virtually no one understood how fragile John was, particularly since he was playing some of his best hockey as a Leaf under the team's new coach, Doug Carpenter. He also resumed his habit of riding in limousines to nightclubs around the city, although he favored Paparizzi's, a club not unlike the now-defunct L'arnaque II. As it had at Larnaque's, John's celebrity gained him easy entry past the beefy doormen and attracted the kind of party favors he had grown accustomed to in Montreal. Located up Highway 404, at Highway 7, the club was out of reach—and out of mind—of the Leafs' management and influence.

Close enough to Leafdom to catch all the gossip about John, Mauro was nonplussed by what was being said about the hockey player. Like Labonte, he cherished John's charm and wit. He rarely accompanied John on his nightly excursions but the few times he'd seen John drug-addled had shocked him. On one such occasion, John had stood on a balcony half-naked, clutching his body in horror: he was experiencing the sensation of bugs crawling under his skin. This phenomenon, known as "cocaine bugs," is a condition related to ingestion of heavy doses (John, by this time, was taking up to three grams of cocaine a day).

Although the press got wind of John's bizarre behavior, the stories never reported the rumors of his drug use. Speculating about drug use had always been considered outside the realm of regular beat reporting. Throughout NHL history, stories about players' drug- or alcohol-related excesses had been passed down, like folklore, but rarely reported on, until a death was involved. The league had weathered the bombshell 1986 *Sports Illustrated* story describing cocaine use among at least five Edmonton Oilers chiefly because the story did not name names. This fact lessened the impact—at least in the eyes of Oilers' management, who dismissed the allegations as groundless "witch hunting." It was Borje Salming's 1986 admission of cocaine use to *The Toronto Star* that finally exploded the myth that hockey players were impervious to the drug culture. Salming was suspended eight games under the NHL's zero-tolerance drug policy. This policy had previously been used against only two players (Don Murdoch and Rick Natress), which left the impression that they were each isolated incidents.

Even though John's drug use escaped mention in the papers, the effects of it on his behavior increased the hockey player's newsworthiness.

• • •

Mauro leaped from his kitchen chair to answer his phone. It was John, his voice doleful, like that of a frightened child's.

"Cheech, I fucked up, I smashed the 'Vette. Can you help me?"

"Where are you?"

"I don't know, Danforth and Logan, you'll see the cop cars."

By the time Mauro reached John, a large crowd had gathered, drawn by the number of police cruisers, which seemed abnormally high for a fender bender. Photographers had already snapped pictures of John in the passenger seat of a cruiser for the next day's front pages.

Later, as they drove back to North Toronto, Mauro told John "the boys" on the force had told him that Kordic was being watched. John promised he would clean up his act.

John wrecked his Corvette again in January of 1990.

John had proven he could be an effective player when his concentration was intact. Doug Carpenter, who had been hired over the summer to replace George Armstrong, produced more from John than any Leaf coach before him. He simply gave John a regular shift and an assignment on the power play, which generated positive results.

At the halfway point in the season, the press traditionally rated the Leafs under a mock report-card system. John rated a B-minus, with the boast of "a 20-goal season looming." He was also indispensable since Carpenter had no other players to counter heavyweights like Basil McRae, Bob Probert, and Wayne Van Dorp in the Norris Division.

Carpenter considered Toronto a premiere post. He teamed with Floyd Smith, who succeeded Gord Stellick as general manager, to bring the first stability to the Gardens in almost ten years. He had originally been hired in 1984 by Punch Imlach to coach the Leafs' AHL team in St. Catharines. He led the Saints to a 43–31–6 record, then was unexpectedly let go. He resurfaced in coaching the next season, with the New Jersey Devils. That club improved under Carpenter to 64 points from 42 the previous season.

Carpenter's door was always open to John. The coach's open-door policy was more than hospitality. John often chatted for hours on end simply because he had nowhere to go. Sometimes, Carpenter had to adjust his schedule to accommodate John, but he felt it was a fair price to pay if it kept Kordic off the streets. They talked like old school buddies, and John had "a million stories," Carpenter would say, about his experiences on and off the ice. Carpenter also encouraged Larivierre and Mike Kitchen to foster big-brotherly relationships with John. The arrangements were meant to be a survival guide: for John and the coaches, who had no idea how far John might take them all.

John, his own worst enemy, fell into familiar self-destructive patterns. Captain Rob Ramage, who was assigned to be John's roommate on the road, chastised John on several occasions before reporters. His patience was approaching saturation, and one time during practice, he was so incensed with John's moribund work ethic, he swatted a water bottle with his stick. Carpenter's patience was similarly tested and he snapped at John once, telling him to "just leave" the ice if he wasn't interested in what the team was doing.

Most of the team's appreciation of John as a player became clouded by their growing lack of respect for him on a personal level. Only a handful of Leafs really knew the degree of John's focus on the game. John often glanced over at Kotsopoulos before games and smirked, which meant, "I own the real estate tonight." Other times, his hands would be too battered to be used as weapons. Then he would look at Kotsopoulos and simply shake his head. He also tried to make everyone laugh with his repertoire of one-liners. (Once, while sitting on a stationary bike, and with the press scrummed around Carpenter in earnest, he noticed the Flintstones on an overhead television set and blurted out, "Who would you rather fuck, Wilma or Betty?") Then he would take to heart a newspaper poll listing him as the city's least favorite athlete. During a practice the next day, he lined up along the boards for a

Even as a rookie, John's reputation was as one of the most feared fighters.

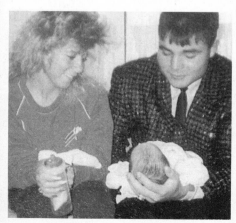

With fiancée Sandy Bernard, John cradles her newly born godchild, Nicole.

The traditional head shave made rookies easy to spot at the 1986 Canadiens training camp. John, in the middle, is all smiles with Shane Corson (right) and Dave Malley.

TORONTO STAR FILE PHOTO

John was a frequent visitor to the Montreal offices of NHL executive vice-president Brian O'Neil. He is accompanied by Canadiens coach Jean Perron after the infamous February 23, 1987 brawl with Quebec's Gord Donnelly.

BILL GRIMSHAW/CP

In this 1987 shot, Perron orders John—who often clashed with his coaches—off the Forum ice during practice.

ALLEN McINNIS/CP

On February 18, 1990, John's antics were enjoyed by all at a sledge-hockey game to benefit the MacMillan Rehabilitation Centre in Toronto. John gladly gave his time to benefit the handicapped.

BERNARD WEIL/TORONTO STAR

Regina came to Toronto to live with John after a series of personal setbacks led to his mysterious absence from a Leafs game March 3, 1990.

John was good friends with Michel Labonte, a Montreal kick-boxer and night club owner. Here, he is at ease with Michel's 16-year-old son, Steve, hours after both were involved in a street fight during a 1991 riot in Montreal.

John's days as a Maple Leaf were numbered after his demotion to Newmarket in November 1990. Here, he is hoisting weights under the guidance of Saints coach Frank Anzalone.

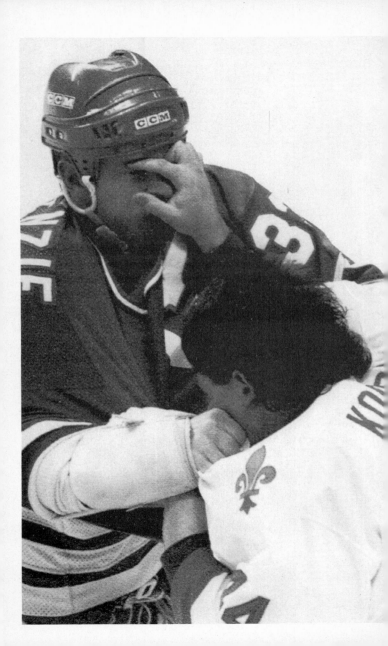

John and his best friend, Bryan Fogarty, shared a Quebec condo in September 1991. The press had a field day playing up the fact that the two were also recovering alcoholics.
JACQUES BOSSINOT/CP

John's brother, Dan, who played with the Philadelphia Flyers, supports Regina Kordic after the church service for John's funeral.
IAN SCOTT/EDMONTON JOURNAL

Left
John squared off regularly with several NHL enforcers, including Hartford's Jim McKenzie in this October 1991 shot taken at the Nordiques home opener at the Colisee in Quebec City.
JACQUES BOSSINOT/CP

Nancy Masse—whom John had planned to marry—was dogged by the press during the inquest.

LEOPOLD ROUSSEAU

Regina Kordic sits with lawyer Paul Bouchard at the inquest in Quebec City.

JACQUES BOSSINOT/CP

drill, and shouted up to agent Sam Nestico, "Sammy, get me the fuck outta here." For several moments afterward, there was an uncomfortable silence on the ice.

In late February 1990, John was again in his fast-forward social mode. During a team dinner in Vancouver—the annual freebie in which the team gathered at an expensive restaurant and left the rookies to foot the bill—24 team members ran up a $1,534 tab at Joe Fortes Seafood House and stuck Scott Pearson and John McIntyre with it.

During the meal, John and goalie Allan Bester traded barbs. Then, in an instant, John flew from his chair and rocked him with a blow to the head.

"I don't need your help, I don't need anyone," John yelled before bolting from the table.

Todd Gill rose to follow him, then Rob Ramage.

In his room afterward, John phoned Mauro back in Toronto.

"Cheech, I just punched Allan Bester in the face."

"You what . . ."

"He was being a little prick so I cuffed him one."

When he returned from the road trip, John began sleeping at Nikki Kruze's house in Markham. Kruze, an exotic dancer, was John's friend and the only native Edmontonian he knew in Toronto. Magic was always nearby, and John was hanging out with other people, too, people he met in VIP booths at Paparizzi's.

On Friday, March 2, he fought twice in the first half of a rough contest in Detroit, then played only one shift throughout the remainder of the game. A limousine whisked him away when the team arrived back in Toronto.

He returned to Mauro's home on March 3. Nobody was in. He had a pocketful of powder, and everywhere he looked, he saw Sandy. Things hadn't been going well between them. She wasn't returning his phone calls.

He looked at the clock. He had been up all night, probably the night before, but he couldn't remember. He was exhausted. Sleep came easily to him. Sleep took away all the confusion.

Four miles away, the Leafs were in their dressing room. By the time John woke up, the Detroit Red Wings were almost dressed. Players were stretching. Warm-ups were about 15 minutes away.

John grabbed the phone, pivoting out from under the covers. He stood, in his underwear. He knew Carpenter's direct number. He had his words in his mind, he was too sick to make it, he said. Before anyone could reply, he hung up.

The phone rang back almost immediately. He let it ring. He walked away so he couldn't hear it. Then he picked it up and began dialing friends.

Magic was at home, watching the game on television. Early on in the first period, his cellular phone rang.

"Hey buddy, you gotta set something up for later."

"John, where are you?"

"I'm here man, wait a minute . . . ah, there's some fuckin' guys at my door from the Leafs . . . I don't wanna talk to them."

"John, tell me where you are right now."

"I'm hiding behind the couch, I don't wanna talk to no one."

The press gathered in droves at the Gardens the next day. John strode in wearing a black T-shirt with the word Team stenciled on it. He kept tight-lipped until he emerged from a meeting with Smith. "I'm through . . . I'm gone," he said.

Smith had told John that the hockey player had crossed the line, and the Leafs had no other option but to trade him. The NHL's trading deadline was March 6. John left with the understanding that if the right deal was offered, he'd be playing in another city.

Before the afternoon was over, John met with Carpenter. He told the coach he wanted to apologize to his teammates, and he phoned Ramage to convey the same message.

When John got home, dozens of cameras and gawkers

were there to receive him. John's plight was one of the hottest news items in the city. There was intense interest in his story. The *Toronto Star* managed to arrange an interview with John at a nearby restaurant where, inside, a woman wished him luck and asked for an autograph for her son, while outside, a cabbie asked him to sign a blank envelope for his girlfriend. John said he was heartbroken over the prospect of leaving Toronto. He didn't want the fans to hate him. "To leave now would be running away from what I've done." He grew defiant. "My problems are personal; they are not drug-related . . . I have heard the rumors, people speculating this and that, but I want to put this to rest."

Carpenter was preparing to leave his office at the Gardens. He tidied up some papers, but his mind was elsewhere, with John. He was convinced that he'd done his best on John's behalf. Larivierre and Kitchen deserved a lot of credit, as well. They had tried to get Kordic the help he needed, had sent John to Humewood House (a drug and alcohol abuse rehab center in Toronto), had the team doctors work with him, all to no avail. One specialist left in disgust seconds after being introduced to John in the Gardens' executive offices: when John heard the man's name, he'd said, "That's Portuguese, eh? I thought Portuguese guys clean toilets around here."

Carpenter had told the press as much as he could, as much as he dared. Privately, he'd felt all along John had a drug problem, had even discussed it with his assistant coaches and the general manager. He had decided against approaching the league. He was determined to preserve the player's career.

Carpenter walked out into the quiet corridor leading to the arena's Church Street exits. He had done his best, but he knew he couldn't deal with a dedicated cocaine addict.

Chapter Twenty

REGINA KORDIC, dressed in widow's black, came to visit John in Toronto, and stayed with him in Mauro's North Toronto duplex. It wasn't very long before John's mother knew about his drug use. From the moment she found out, Regina regimented John's life. She expected John's full compliance. She trusted no one with John, except Mauro's girlfriend, Leslie Cotto. John acquiesced sheepishly at first. For several days, his demons subdued, he had no contact with any drugs.

Regina told Cotto many heart-warming stories about John's childhood. She repeatedly referred to her "Johnny," and how she didn't understand what was happening to him. Regina even shed light on the improbable angularity of John's jawline: John, at age five, managed to drive away in his father's car, smashing it into a wall and breaking his jaw on impact.

Cotto admired the older woman's strength. She'd caught glimpses of this same strength in John, when he wasn't struggling with his demons.

John drove to the Gardens to apologize to his teammates. The players watched as, downcast, standing before them, John spoke in a monotone, visibly forcing back his emotions. He asked for their forgiveness, for their forbearance.

He said he had personal problems, that he was working on them. He assured them that he wouldn't repeat his mistakes.

The trade deadline passed without any player movement on the Leafs front. Smith wasn't going to give John away without fair value in return. He had phone calls with Edmonton, Washington, and Quebec, but all were interested in package deals only: John and a top-flight Leaf like Vince Damphousse. None wanted John solo. By now, John's problems were well-known throughout the NHL, and the press speculated that, without the Leafs, Kordic's career was over. In a surprising confluence of events, John began practicing with the Leafs again, despite Smith's announcement that the player was suspended without pay indefinitely. The press began digging into the apparent conflict, and discovered that—according to an agreement between the NHL and its players' union—a suspended player's pay cannot be withheld indefinitely, providing the player remains with the team.

Player union executive director Alan Eagleson checked communiqués from the league and told the press there was no record of John's suspension in their files. "What does this mean?" Eagleson said in a *Toronto Star* story. "It means that Kordic cannot oblige the Leafs to play him, of course. But it also means he can oblige them to pay him in accordance with his contract. They can drop him from the team. That's their option. But he must be paid."

After the trade deadline, Edmonton general manager Glen Sather commented on his belief that Smith "wasn't all that interested" in trading John.

The *Toronto Star* postulated that Smith and Carpenter had concocted the suspension as a way of scaring John straight. In between Smith's comments and press speculation, it became clear that NHL teams kept enforcers around for as long as they were able to walk their violent beats.

Dave Schultz, the famous "Hammer" of the Philadelphia Flyers' Broad Street Bullies days in the mid 1970s, empathized with John. In an interview with the *Star*'s Milt Dunnell, at the height of the controversy, Schultz stated: "I still watch hockey on TV and I see people in the goon or enforcer role—whatever you want to call it—and I know nobody really appreciates their problems. I've had the experience of hearing 17,000 fans yelling, 'We want Schultz.' I knew they were not expecting a goal . . . but not one enforcer ever got any kind of recognition [except fines and suspensions] from the NHL. If enforcers were not needed in hockey, the clubs would not have them. John Ferguson was as much responsible for the successes of the Montreal Canadiens as anyone else, but did he ever get elected to the hall of fame? Freddie Shero [former Flyers coach] would be quoted as saying after we won the Stanley Cup, that, 'Without Schultzie, we wouldn't have been there.' Bobby Clarke got to the hall of fame but I didn't. I'm going to sound facetious now but I'm suggesting we [enforcers] should have our own hall of fame."

On March 25, 1989, three weeks after missing the Detroit game, John was back in the lineup as the Leafs marched towards the play-offs. They would compile a 72-point season, and put on a game showing in the play-offs before bowing out in the second round.

John moved in with Sandy when he returned to Edmonton for the offseason. Much of the outlandish musculature he had packed on in Montreal was gone.

He took up with his old circle of friends—Walsh, Lemaire, Senregret. He was out in the bars again, mostly for something to do. Barry T's was still a hot spot in the suburbs, and John gladly stepped in as guest bartender when called upon.

He also took up with Raj Samarval. The two had met when they were in their mid teens. Samarval was one of dozens of good soccer players in the city who had raved to everyone about a dynamite 18-year-old goalie named John Kordic. Their paths crossed again playing shinny hockey and ball hockey at the Westmount arena, which was near the Kordic house. Samarval's parents owned two Dairy Queen franchises, and encouraged their son's interest in horses. Samarval owned several, including Newer Entrepreneur, and often made gentlemanly bets with Glenn Anderson of the Edmonton Oilers, who owned a horse named Scurryon. Samarval invited John to watch some of his standardbreds, maybe place a bet or two. Kevin McClelland and Craig MacTavish also owned horses, and they, along with Mark Messier, dropped by periodically to check out the action. Samarval guided John through the complicated business of reading programs and picking winners. Two years earlier, they had successfully bet a Win-4 and cashed a winner's ticket for $28,000.

Samarval was not a stranger to John's belligerence. In 1988, he'd witnessed a confrontation between the Canadian heavyweight boxing champion, Ken Lakusta, and John. Lakusta had been standing near the bar at Barry T's. Two men who had been talking with Sandy suddenly began swearing at her. Samarval speculates that she threw a drink at one of them in response to a lewd comment. John was about to confront the men, when Lakusta bolted towards John, insisting that Sandy had started the incident. He also described her, from head to foot, with vitriol, and told John the fair fight was with him, not with the two men. John challenged Lakusta to face him outside. Patrons stampeded for the exits in anticipation of the titanic bout.

Outside, they glared at each other, but that was as far as they got to fighting. Friends on both sides pulled the two apart.

One night, near the end of April 1989, John and Samarval ended up in the back of a paddy wagon, charged with disturbing the peace after a brawl at Barry T's. (In July they would both respond to the charges in court. John's charges were later dropped when he paid $1,500 as restitution for the door he'd damaged at the bar.)

By the first of May. John was two weeks away from a trip to Tucson, Arizona, and the Sierra clinic for drug and alcohol rehabilitation. He had consented, in the face of ultimatums from his family, the Leafs, and his agent Sam Nestico, to get professional help.

He was told he would not have a career with the Leafs if he failed.

Chapter Twenty-one

ON MAY 14, 1990, Sandy drove John to Henwood, the Edmonton chapter of the Alberta Alcohol and Drug Abuse Commission (AADAC). John balked at entering a rehab center, but he knew he had to comply with demands made on him to seek professional help. As they walked into the facility, a car roared up to the sidewalk. An old man, obviously intoxicated, stumbled out of the passenger door. A woman came around from the driver's side, flung a suitcase on the ground beside him, and snapped, "I don't want you home until you sober up."

They sat in a office that reminded Sandy of a doctor's office. The old man, liquor on his breath, was sitting beside them. He insisted they look at a series of Polaroids he pulled from his pocket. A man who said he was a transvestite came into the office, wailing, whimpering that he was going to die. Welcome to AADAC.

John was still locked on a high. A nurse asked him what he had taken. He replied cocaine. A counselor recommended that John report for sessions. John agreed, attended twice, then abandoned the sessions. He told Sandy and his family that he was quitting, and didn't require any further help.

John was discharged from AADAC May 16, 1990. On June 28, a complete report of his assessment, treatment, prognosis, and recommendations was included in a discharge document sent to Don Meehan and Patrick Morris, barristers and solicitors of Newport Sports Management,

John's agents. Actually, John was discharged at the request of AADAC staff. He fought with other patients, a collection of "court-ordered convicts" who he said provoked him into confrontations: a charge backed up by several counselors.

On June 6, John entered his first serious rehabilitation program. He was admitted on an in-patient basis to Sierra Tucson, a highly regarded substance abuse treatment center in Tucson, Arizona.

The extent of John's substance abuse was documented in his discharge report, which was completed at the end of the month and released to Patrick Morris under the protection of U.S. federal confidentiality guidelines.

File number 4703 listed him as patient Kordic, John; it made no mention of the NHL outside a reference to John's career as a professional hockey player. Virtually all entries were based on statements given by John during in-depth interviews, or observations made by counselors and psychologists.

During the preliminary interview, John stated that his entering treatment was precipitated by his cocaine and alcohol abuse. He indicated he was "intervened on [sic] by family and lawyer, was bottom-lined by employer to come into treatment."

Over the course of the interview, he was asked to detail his alcohol- and drug-abuse history. He said that he'd first used alcohol at age 13, and that he drank infrequently. He first used cocaine, he told the interviewer, in 1988. He said he'd ingested three to four grams the night before entering treatment, which categorized him as a "binge user." John became evasive when he was asked to explain his pattern of frequency and the amounts he used.

He also said he had used steroids every year for the last three summers.

John's reflections on his mental health focused on Ivan's death. He reported that he had "unresolved sadness, anger, and shame around his father's death." John said his cocaine use dramatically increased after Ivan passed away. With considerable acuity, John perceived that drugs had replaced Ivan as his support system. As a result of the drug use, he said he experienced "easy fatigability, shortness of breath, sweating, cold hands, dizziness, light-headedness, trouble falling asleep, trouble staying asleep, dry mouth, difficulty concentrating, feeling keyed up and on edge." The symptoms lasted for several hours, and created "problems in his life . . . family and girlfriend did not want to be around me." John said he also became moody, but that his mood was generally depressed, and he lacked interest in his usual activities. His focus was on getting high, then sleeping when he was not using. As a result, he stated feelings of "worthlessness, and guilt with recurrent thoughts of death." Consequently, he began hallucinating, destroying property, then avoiding social contact to stay at home alone and get high.

When the interview turned to the subject of his career, John said he had a history of being violent, and that being the "team heavy" was how he made his living, he was "paid to fight." He also stated that he had a "reputation as being a drugger," and when asked about his post-hockey life, he said, "I have never thought about it." John said he had spent $80,000 on cocaine, and, in the past, used money he had previously put away for his retirement.

Following the preliminary interview, John was assigned to group therapy, and monitored daily. John hated having to face his peers; the entire process of sitting down in a circle of chairs with other patients, stating his name, and talking out his problems irritated him. To him, it was all "rehab," and he detested it.

During his time there, a psychologist administered a battery of three psychoanalytic and indicator tests.

These tests are standard institutional testing instruments, and usher the patient into the clinical aspect of the treatment.

In the first, the Shipley, John was presented with three sections which gauged his responses to vocabulary, abstractions, and conceptual quotient tests. He was then given the Minnesota Multiphasic Personality Inventory, which requires the patient's response to 567 items. The responses are then reviewed against a series of ten scales. In one scale, John's result was listed as an extreme elevation, suggesting "restlessness, agitation, and impatience." The final test was the Incomplete Sentences Blank, the results of which exhibited John's difficulty in relating with others: "People in general are very stupid. Men are all the same—they are pigs." Additional statements included: "I can't understand people at times. My greatest fear is fear. I suffer when others don't understand. I need to be trusted again. This place is boring. I am very impatient with all this. The only trouble is that I am the problem."

John was angry and evasive throughout his stay at Sierra Tucson. He intimidated other patients when they accused him of breaching in-patient conduct codes. He was approached by his counselors, and in a "rap group" session with other patients, he said he had a great deal of anger and couldn't "wait to leave all this bullshit behind." On July 7, he was confronted by other patients and staff for violating patient confidentiality. Entries in his file stated he had participated in a background check on a female in his group, and her husband, violating patient-confidentiality guidelines. He then said jokingly that he was blackmailing the female and presented two love letters to her. The female became angry, and he reacted by splashing her with muddy water.

Following the incident, John was asked to leave the center. His discharge summary was prepared July 9, and sent to Patrick Morris. John completed 21 days in treatment, and it was recommended he continue his recovery process for cocaine addiction at another treatment center, as well as enroll in a 12-step self-help group. The final line of the summary stated: "Prognosis seems poor."

Also included in the discharge document was a summation from a doctor who included among his observations that while in treatment, John's "behavioral contract should include no acting out violent behavior. Historically, his violence has not been unprovoked."

So John was on the outside again, and with essentially nothing resolved. Training camp was two months away.

Surprisingly, despite the clinical recommendation for his continued therapy, the Leafs were going to put John back into a uniform.

Chapter Twenty-two

THE 1990-91 LEAFS training camp had barely begun when John Kordic cracked his cell phone over the head of a black youth who'd called him a homeboy at a Newmarket bar. He wound up at a police station overnight. A few nights later, cameras picked him up in a private box during an exhibition game drinking and cheering goals against the Leafs. When he returned to the dressing room after the game, his bags were already packed for the minors.

Some attributed John's demotion to his antics the previous season. Many believed he had burned all his bridges; John's support system had crumbled under supersaturation. He was left to orbit another team again.

John, feeling like a pariah, informed his agents that he was seeking alternative representation. He enlisted the services of Sam Nestico, a burly man who resembled Jim Belushi. Nestico fell into the role once assumed by Labonte and Mauro. It was Nestico's goal to get John back into the NHL. To this end, he tried to make John understand how important it was for him to change—all to no avail. Kordic wasn't listening. As far as John was concerned, everyone else had the problem, not him.

John was now a member of the Leafs's AHL affiliate, the Newmarket Saints. His most prized possession was his cell phone. He was stranded in a small town, population about 25,000, 35 miles outside of Toronto, whose claim to fame was its Mars Bar factory. John spent a lot of time phoning anyone who could relieve his boredom, or the Leafs' front office, to argue over why they wouldn't advance him money on his salary.

He was under the direction of Saints' coach Frank Anzalone, a newcomer to the Leafs organization. Anzalone, 35, a native New Yorker with a Bronx accent, had posted impressive numbers in seven previous seasons as head coach of the Lake Superior State hockey team. Anzalone's directive from the Leafs' brass was to start from ground zero and reshape a team that wasn't producing any NHL prospects. The team had some wily characters in Doug Shedden, Allan Hepple, Bill Root, and others, who were still in hockey because they loved the game, not because they entertained any notions of winning an NHL scoring title. Root, for example, came to the arena on weekdays after putting in eight or more hours at his construction business.

None of the Saints players were accustomed to Anzalone's rah-rah work ethics and immediately sized him up as a hotshot college coach. He was criticized in the local media for trying to graft methods that may have worked with college players onto players with professional-level egos.

Anzalone established a precedent for hard work as best he could with John. John broke the ice with him while riding a stationary bike. "Hey Frank, I hear you're like Mike Keenan, you're tough on players," John ventured as Anzalone walked by. "Well, John, you know, I do what I have to get my players to perform." "Yeah, well I hate fucking Mike Keenan," John shot back, then smiled.

Anzalone worked hard to help John sort himself out professionally. The coach told John that he was in charge of his own agenda. If he got into shape, he would be that much more desirable to another team. John, clearly absorbing some of the advice, amazed Anzalone in the weight room. Without having touched a weight in almost six months, John hoisted 145 pounds and snapped off 15 seated shoulder presses with apparent ease. John was an asset on the bench for a while, largely because Mike Stevens and Mike Jackson were the only players willing to drop their gloves for the team, and neither was a household name. In his fourth game with the Saints, John scored the winning goal late in the third period of a deadlocked tilt with Maine.

Anzalone called John's stint with the Saints "the John Kordic show [in which] John is the star." But things deteriorated rapidly. By the fourth week of the season, he told Smith that John was clearly no longer interested in being with the team: since the Maine game, he had fought with a teammate on the team bench, spat at a referee, and had been suspended for giving the middle-finger salute to a hostile crowd supporting the Capital District Islanders. Anzalone periodically stopped game films in the darkened dressing room when John's snoring was heard over his voice. "Don't worry, coach, it's John," someone would yell up to him. John kept a running joke with Anzalone, asking facetiously if the Leafs had called him up or some team had made a trade for him. In Toronto, his former number 27 had long since been passed on to Lucien Deblois.

Ultimately, Smith informed John he could no longer practice with the Saints, and that the franchise had stopped paying his tab at the Voyageur, where the hockey player had been staying. John ignored the order at first; he even sought out a reporter to make his defiance public. Within days, though, he met with Smith again and agreed it was time to move on.

Anzalone stoically hid his disappointment over John's fate. It was the same stoicism adopted by the Leafs, and virtually all NHL teams, whenever such decisions are reached. He had railed at John, on several occasions, over his lack of desire and work ethics. His own players, though, eventually took him aside: "Leave him alone, Frank," he was told. "Just dress him, that's all he wants." Long after John was gone, Anzalone continued to argue anyone down who challenged his belief that somewhere inside John was a 20-goal scorer in the NHL who was as tough as anyone who played the game.

John vanished for a couple of days. During a morning practice, though, he dropped in undetected to gather his belongings. Anzalone was having a chalk board meeting on the ice when suddenly John interrupted, walking and sliding over the ice with a large pizza. He began handing out slices to the players, his way of saying goodbye. With nowhere to go and virtually no one to turn to, John, depressed and desperate, went to stay with his old friend from Edmonton, Nikki Kruze.

On January 24, 1991, Smith traded John Kordic and Paul Fenton to the Washington Capitals for future considerations, which turned out to be a fifth-round draft pick. John, who had long since left Kruze's hospitality behind, contacted Howard Gourwitz, a Detroit-based lawyer who agreed to represent John and get his career back on track. Gourwitz put John up in his house, arranged for John to work out with a local junior team, then began working the phones, telling NHL general managers John had turned himself around. Gourwitz arranged a meeting between John and Chicago coach and general manager Mike Keenan. Keenan, already disenchanted with tough guys Stu Grimson and Mike Peluso, and fully aware of John's reputation, wasn't convinced that John would fit in.

A deal with Chicago never materialized, and Smith was upset over the apparent breach of the league's rules against tampering with a signed player. John, though, had cleared waivers back in November. When the Washington trade was consummated, there wasn't a stampede for John's services.

Prior to the trade, the Capitals were at the Joe Louis Arena for a game against the Red Wings. At the game, John met with Washington coach Terry Murray, director of player personnel Jack Button, and general manager David Poile, in an attempt to acquit himself. After John's speech, Poile decided to give John a chance to redeem himself. Poile returned to the Capitals' dressing room to tell his players about the trade. He told them their lack of aggressiveness was contributing to their losing record, and he also asked his players to report any aberrant behavior by John.

When the trade was announced in Washington, Poile knew he would have to rationalize the apparent folly of acquiring a known problem child, even if it had been for next to nothing. "One wrong move and John's out of here in a second," he told reporters. "We're taking a small risk in terms of what we've given up to get John . . . but let's be honest, if we were in first place right now rather than fifth, we'd have never made the deal. He's very definitely a man on a bubble."

The deal meant John would be teammates again with Al Iafrate and former Montreal defenseman Mike Lalor. After a week's practice, John played his first game against the New York Islanders and fought Mitch Vukota. He threw his fists with his now-classic aplomb, recklessly, from all angles. His assaults, though, no longer possessed that savage level of strength that had formerly hammered respect into his foes. At best, he was given draws in his bouts. Tie Domi surprised him with his own reckless abandon, and quickly had John on the ice, on his back.

John's willingness to enter the ring for his new teammates earned him kudos from the press. The players saw the benefits in having John, a player who would punch and take punches for them, without fail. It was no coincidence that the Capitals went 4–0–1 in John's first five games.

John was also called on by the press to answer questions about his checkered past. He played true to form by providing usable quotes: "That's all in the past," he said. "I'd call this my last chance . . . it didn't happen here, it can't happen here, and it won't happen here."

On February 12, 1991, Lalor and several Capitals were milling about their dressing room after practice. It was still morning, and they were due for a lunch-hour visit with disabled children at a local hospital. John would have joined them, but he'd failed to show up for practice. There was immediate concern for John's well-being. Most NHL players are extremely supportive when one of their teammates has problems. Lalor told the other players that he would drive across town to check on John.

The drive from the Capital Centre Arena to John's one-bedroom apartment in Bowie, Maryland, can be an arduous one in traffic. When John opened his door, Lalor knew something was wrong. He spent the next 15 minutes trying to convince John he was his friend, and to let him in.

"John, are you okay? The guys were wondering why you missed practice today."

"I don't know . . . it's weird . . . this isn't my place, this isn't my apartment."

Lalor's eyes followed John to the curtains, where he appeared to be hiding as he looked out the window.

"Are you on something, John?" he asked.

"No, no . . . nothing's wrong, don't worry about it."

Lalor suggested they go get something to eat. John complied, and when they returned an hour and a half later, Lalor stayed with John. There was a knock at the door. Coach Murray and assistant coach Terry Perpitch were standing in the hallway. This time, John opened the door without hesitation.

John assumed his customary, expressionless countenance and denied his substance abuse. He had an arsenal of explanations, which he had mastered over the years. His easy answers and rehearsed phrases couldn't hide the state he was in. Kordic had nowhere to run, nowhere to hide.

Stories the next day said that John had admitted he was an alcoholic. For the first time in his career, he'd broken down and confessed to his problem. Murray and Poile told the media the hockey player would be receiving professional help. Poile was not forthcoming with information about what help John was receiving; he only indicated John's treatment had begun. The Capitals were scheduled to take a week-long road trip; John was left behind in Washington. He was admitted as a patient at a local hospital and began a series of tests and sessions with a psychologist. After his assessment, John was enrolled in a local chapter of Alcoholics Anonymous.

Poile said John's admission "hit me like a shot between the eyes." While on the road trip, he met with his players and discussed John's problems. It was decided that John deserved a second chance, but it would be put to a player vote. John's new teammates gave him an immeasurable show of support by voting him back into the lineup. John's return to the lineup was set for a March 3 game against the New York Rangers. Then, in a sad turn of events, John missed a preceding weekend game in what was described as another alcohol-related incident. He was suspended immediately and indefinitely, his hockey career no longer an option. Ironically, this no-show was almost a year to the day after his infamous no-show at Maple Leaf Gardens for a game against Detroit.

John sat in the press box while Poile pondered his next move. As he watched his teammates skate to a 4–4 draw against the Rangers, he told a reporter: "It's a day-to-day thing . . . Today, I've beaten it today, but I haven't beaten it today; I haven't gone to bed yet. We tied a gamer here, 4–4. The guys are going to want to go out and have a bite to eat and a few drinks. So far today, I've beaten it. So far, since I've been out, I've beaten it. It's a daily thing, it's a daily battle and tomorrow's another day and another battle."

Poile wasn't about to give up on John. The general manager had plans to get John into treatment with a prominent drug therapist, Dr. James Fearing, at the famous Hazelden clinic in Minnesota.

Poile told the media only that John had fallen off the wagon and was going to receive professional help for a problem with alcohol. The general manager also refrained from comment, public or otherwise, about the possibility of John's dependence on drugs. Like Savard and Carpenter before him, he was in a Catch-22 situation: he had to live up to the league's zero-tolerance policy regarding drug use, but also felt he had to preserve a young man's career.

The Capitals fully assumed the costs of sending John to Hazelden where he was placed under James Fearing's care.

Chapter Twenty-three

JOHN CAME to Hazelden, the health facility dedicated to helping the chemically dependent, in early May after leaving Washington. For the first time in his experiences with rehab, John seemed a willing participant. At the end of May, however, Dr. Fearing moved him to a halfway house in St. Paul because John was having difficulty participating in group sessions; he was never open enough with other patients, choosing to keep his demons to himself. To keep him motivated, Fearing arranged for John to work part-time at a gym. In addition, he thought it would be a good idea to get the recovering players seats to the Stanley Cup play-off round between the Minnesota North Stars and the Edmonton Oilers.

Glen Sonmor, a former Minnesota North Star and recovering alcoholic, regularly joined the players who were in therapy for chemical dependence. He often picked John up from the halfway house on his way to AA meetings in the Twin Cities. Each night, there were dozens of such meetings across the area, which earned it the reputation as the recovery hub of America. He brought John to the Eden Prairie Mall, where large AA meetings were held, usually with a guest speaker. At first, John listened most of the time; then he began to open up at smaller meetings of about 15 to 20 people. He wore a name tag with John K. written on it and sat with people around a table. When it was his turn to speak, he said, "My name is John, I'm an alcoholic."

John spoke about how he made it through the day in his battle to keep a safe distance from alcohol. Like other people at the meetings, he was encouraged to talk, freely and confidently, about how many alcohol-free days he had notched. There were no group leaders, only speakers. John was also presented with the 12 self-help steps prescribed by AA, which would take him the rest of his life to successfully complete. At the end of the meetings, an AA member would ask if anyone present was celebrating an anniversary. They would be given coins to commemorate, incrementally, periods of clean living, usually after three months, then six months, and so on. The coins were also inscribed with self-help messages, reminders of the spiritual commitment needed to win the daily battles and ultimately the war on alcohol dependency. The back side of the coin read: "God grant me the serenity to accept the things I cannot change, the courage to change the things I can, and the wisdom to know the difference." On the front, it read: "To thine own self be true." The front of the coin was emblazoned with a triangle which was framed by the words "Service, Recovery, Unity"—the three words of motivation of the AA recovery program. Inside the triangle was a Roman numeral totaling the number of sober days the coin holder had completed. As a bond to all that the coin stood for, each person was asked to carry it with them always, wherever they went and whatever they did.

John left Hazelden, the halfway house, and Minnesota in June, before he completed anything he was enrolled in. Another player in the program, Link Gaetz, also dropped out a short while after John. Sonmor heard stories of John and Gaetz heading out into the night, breaking the rules in the 12 steps of self-help. He heard of how John playfully jumped up on a parked car and wound up crashing through the front windshield.

Before he left rehab, John met and became good friends with Bryan Fogarty, the wonderfully talented Quebec Nordiques defenseman who was recovering from his own problems at a Twin Cities halfway house. Fogarty, who was also under Fearing's care, agreed to speak to Nords general manager Pierre Page on John's behalf. John's contract with the Capitals had expired at the end of June and he already knew it wouldn't be renewed. When John left Minnesota before the end of his rehab program, he sealed that fate.

John had been at a play-off game in Minnesota with the other players when he met Poile between periods. Poile was impressed with John's apparent level of fitness. He said John had never looked better, and asked how his treatment was progressing. John was enthusiastic about his progress. He told Poile "they" even handed out "these coins" as a kind of trophy for personal accomplishments. When John reached into his pocket to show Poile the coin, his hand came up empty. There was a moment of silence from John, then an explanation that he must have left it in another pair of jeans. Poile, who knew about the coin's significance, was silent, too. He would never forget that picture of John.

John confounded Poile, Gourwitz, and many of his Capitals teammates when he bolted from his treatment. Gourwitz told reporters he didn't think John was employable until he had "cleaned up his life." By then, Gourwitz had lost regular contact with him. Instead, John phoned Fred Simpson, a Montreal-based agent with a reputation for taking on troubled players that other agents avoided. Simpson neatly fit the bill for John since he had already returned to Montreal and his old room at Labonte's apartment. It was July; by the end of the month, John would be in Quebec for a meeting with Page.

On the Canada Day weekend of 1991, John was already comfortably settled into Labonte's residence. He spent much of his time working out with weights, with a heavy bag, and in the ring with Labonte. He frequently teased Labonte about street fighting, boasting how he would handle his pal in a matter of seconds if Labonte was man enough to oblige him. John had assumed his old attitude, the cockiness that was his edge as a player. It seemed to resurface in Montreal—more than in any other city. John referred to Montreal as "his town," and three years after

the Canadiens' trade, he was still a popular and easily recognized figure on the streets.

The Wednesday before the long weekend, several police
officers had chased a young black man through a run-
down neighborhood and into a dead-end alley. In a confused exchange, they killed the youth with a bullet to the
head. Within hours, it was learned that the youth was un-
armed and had been mistaken for a drug dealer. The police
officers who had killed the young man were hauled onto
the carpet to explain their actions, which to many people,
particularly minorities, appeared to be racially motivated.
Race relations between the police and minorities, never
very good, became worse. The city was alive with racial
tension. In some parts of Montreal, swarms of black and
white youths roamed the streets, vandalizing property,
looking for trouble.

On July 4, John heard shouting and swearing from beneath the balcony of Labonte's first-floor apartment. Suddenly, there was the sound of bottles smashing against the
side of the building.

John moved through the glass sliding doors which
looked out onto the street. He saw Labonte's 14-year-old
son, François, in a melee with four black youths. He could
see similar skirmishes erupting all around the neighborhood. Youths were throwing bottles, windows were
smashed, and a car was set on fire. John was barefoot and
in shorts and a rugby shirt. He vaulted the balcony railing
and rushed into the scene. In an instant, François's attack-
ers noticed John's state of undress and broke bottles
around his feet. In pain, John ran back to the balcony, his
feet bleeding. Seconds later, he stormed back into the fight
wielding a baseball bat. François was lost in a swarm of
eight youths. They saw John approaching, and quickly released François to beat a hasty retreat. John chased them,
then returned to François. Riot police arrived on the scene
to restore order. They kept John and François for several
hours afterward, taking statements.

François was treated for minor cuts and bruises. Later,
he told John the youths began swearing at him and his
girlfriend, and when he returned the vitriol, he was pelted
with rocks and bottles.

The next day, John was featured in stories about the incident. A picture of him with his arm around François's shoulder was carried on the national wire by Canadian Press. Descriptions of John's part in the melee made references to his personal problems and to his role as an enforcer. It was as if he had played a game that night, and the media was still hung up on whether to call him a goon or a hero.

Chapter Twenty-four

DAVE CHAMBERS, the Quebec Nordiques coach and former York University professor, was a month away from the Nords training camp when he took a call at his Georgian Bay cottage. It was general manager Pierre Page at the other end of the line. He suspected he might not enjoy the news he was about to hear. Page confirmed his suspicions when he explained that Quebec had signed John Kordic to a tryout contract.

Chambers immediately voiced his disapproval. He had been an NHL coach for a single season, but was aware of John's reputation. Moreover, he hadn't been consulted.

Throughout 1990–91—Chambers's first season—Page, team owner Marcel Aubut, and the rest of the Nords brass were anxious to land junior-hockey phenomenon Eric Lindros. The Nords held the lucky ticket to the first overall pick in the 1991 draft, since the team had the dubious distinction of owning the NHL's worst record. Lindros was the obvious first overall pick. Destiny had delivered into the Nords' lap one of the greatest prospects ever to play the game. Their would-be victory, however, was scuttled in advance by the Lindros camp, which steadfastly refused to have him report to Quebec. Lindros and his parents snubbed the Nords in May at the Memorial Cup awards banquet in Quebec City, walking right past Aubut, Page, and Chambers without even a nod. The Lindros camp stated that if the Nords still insisted on drafting him, Eric would not put on the Quebec jersey at the draft in June in

Quebec City. Aubut remained undaunted. He negotiated for several hours with Lindros's parents and his agent just to have Eric carry the Nords jersey back to his seat. Less than two months later, with Page on the phone to Chambers, the Nords finally conceded to Lindros and traded him to Philadelphia.

Page's rationale behind signing John was, in part, to counter the loss of Lindros. The franchise had promised its fans that changes were forthcoming: Lindros was to be the focal point of the team's new direction. The Nords suffered another blow when star Russian defenseman Valeri Kamensky broke his leg and was lost for the upcoming season. But the team still intended on giving the fans a name they could talk about, a name that would put "asses" in the seats. By the time Chambers was made aware of John, there were stories ready for print in the Quebec media about the Nords acquiring one of the toughest enforcers ever to play the game.

After his initial disapproval, Chambers slowly came round to the prospect of having John in training camp. His better judgment told him to maintain a balancing act with his general manager. He was still new to the scene, a coach with the league's worst record in his first season at the helm. He had never before administered a hockey team in partnership with a general manager. The desired effect, he thought, was to look as if he was cooperating while keeping a handle on control of the players.

Page met John for the signing at Fogarty's apartment in a trendy St. Foy condominium.

John was made to understand that his contract was contingent on random drug testing. He was required to appear at a testing laboratory in 20 minutes or less from the time he was notified of a test. He was to be paid by the game, $1,500 if he played, $1,000 if he didn't, and a $150,000 bonus awaited him if he stayed clean for the duration of the season. There were 84 games in the Nords schedule.

Page stressed that John was not expected to play every game. He appealed to John to share his experiences with the younger players. The paramount incentive, though, was the financial package.

Page had been swayed to sign John as a result of conversations he'd had with Fogarty, who divulged John's plight to the general manager after he and the hockey player became friends at Hazelden. Fogarty insisted that John could be an asset to the team, and even offered to room with him. Page also consulted Dr. Fearing, who said that the special battles fought by recovering alcoholics could be bolstered by such an arrangement. Fearing also told Page if John could manage to stay sober and drug-free for three months, he had a better than 80 percent chance of recovery. The press smirked at the prospect of two recovering alcoholics rooming together, but Page responded by giving John the incentive of earning $234,000, without playing a single game.

Page sold the contract and the entire idea of signing John to the front office, which jumped on board once they were convinced there was a sufficient safety net in place. It was agreed that John would supply a urine sample for testing, and that he could be asked for a sample on a daily basis. John was given the luxury of forgiveness for a first-time failure; a second failure meant automatic dismissal. The contract also carried a clause that enabled the team to terminate the contract at any time.

John was brought before one of the leading accountancy firms in North America—Samson, Belair, Deloit, and Touche—who were to help sort out his confused financial affairs. Among his many outstanding debts, John owed repair costs to an Edmonton rental car agency for almost writing off a Nissan 300ZX, and was being sought by a Toronto bank which had extended him a personal line of credit. Most of John's outstanding financial problems were remedied, free of charge, as a result of the firm's relationship with Nords vice president Jean De Legeault.

Once John settled in, Page became like a big brother to him. They met as often as possible for breakfast. Sometimes they would order something to eat, but mostly they would drink coffee and talk.

John and Fogarty, too, leaned on each other, like broth-

ers. They even followed each other numerically in the
lineup, Fogarty wearing number 43 and John number 44.

The two went out to nightclubs on the Grand Allée, the
charming strip of night life running along the south border
of the Quebec legislature buildings. They sipped soft
drinks and smoked cigarettes while everyone around them
partied. Anyone who read the newspapers knew both
players were being tested.

Much of the revelry on the avenue flowed in and out of
the Chez Dagobear disco. It was one of a row of bars and
restaurants, each an architectural masterpiece, that at one
time served as office buildings to the city's most successful
businessmen. John met a beautiful young woman there
named Nancy Masse and asked her to dance. He was sure
he had fallen in love. And he proceeded to do everything
he could to keep her nearby.

John became preoccupied with thoughts of her. But
Nancy was not easy to win over. She didn't trust hockey
players. Eventually, however, she gave in to John, and fell
in love with him.

John stopped by a mirror on his way out of Fogarty's
condo. He filled out his blazer magnificently, and with his
flaring, angled jawline and spiky black hair, he cut a strik-
ing figure. There was nothing he could do about his black
eye, and he didn't want to be late for his first dinner invita-
tion at Nancy's home.

When he arrived, Nancy reached up to kiss him,
proudly, and put her arms around him. John sat down on
the living-room sofa, while Nancy playfully sat across his
lap until he grabbed her, pulling her off balance. Nancy's
sister, Marie-Pierre, was snapping pictures all along.

Nancy's mother and Marie-Pierre's boyfriend were also
enamored of John. All through the house was the smell of
dinner, a beef bourguignonne Nancy had made. Anx-
iously, she scurried from the living room to the kitchen,
checking on dinner, wanting everything to be perfect.

She lit candles as everyone settled into their seats at the
table. Dinner had been perfect, and to make it more so, she
passed around a special sauce she'd prepared using rum as

an ingredient. She was alarmed when John tasted the sauce, and promptly spat out his mouthful.

"I can't eat this, it's got alcohol in it or something," he said. "I'm sorry, but the team is gonna test me, and I can't eat this or I'll fail my test."

Nancy did not agree; she insisted that he not worry about a few mouthfuls.

John remained adamant. The night before, fans had yelled out, *Kor-dic, Kor-dic*—only, in their French accents, the pronunciation was *Kor-dique, Kor-dique*. Initially, he'd thought they were saying Nord-iques, Nord-iques.

For the first time in almost two years, fans were chanting his name again.

Chapter Twenty-five

IT'S THE MIDDLE of the night, and John is careening down the streets of Montreal. When he stops, it's past four in the morning—the same day the Nords are slated to play the Canadiens. Entering the lobby of the Sheraton Hotel, John mistakes the night staff for police informants, and hurls invective at them. Sweating, breathing heavily, he enters the elevator. Fogarty awakes when he hears John come in, looks at his friend's eyes and knows instantly that John is high. John's addled words confirm this.

Although John had not behaved this way in the past, tonight Fogarty saw a new unpredictability in John. His fear mounting by the second, he called Page.

Page came to the room, observed John, and then moved him to another room. Within minutes, Page had found the number to a Montreal laboratory. As soon as it opened, he would have John there to be tested.

Page kept John close to him. He did not want the media finding out.

As John was hustled into a car later that morning, Page pondered the situation. John had been late for practices, and Page had responded by scratching him from the lineup for a road game in New York. John pleaded to go. He didn't want his teammates to think he'd failed a test. There had been tears in his eyes. In the Montreal Sheraton, however, Page had just witnessed a side to John he had not previously seen. John was different, unfathomable.

After the testing, Page told John that he would not be

playing against Montreal that night. John was furious: "That's bullshit, you're fucking me now, you're not going to do this to me now."

"What about our deal, John, we have to look out for you. We want you to straighten up because you have a history and we have to be careful."

"Why are you doing this to me, you can't do this to me, this is my town."

Page would not budge.

Page's role as the purveyor of John's last chance in the NHL was fast crumbling. He had begun to question the wisdom of that role, as well as the inadequacies of the league's drug policy. He thought it was ludicrous for any team to sign John without a policy that required players to come forward and admit to drug problems without fear of reprisal. He admired the National Basketball Association for including that option in its drug policy. Page recalled how Doug Carpenter had told Chambers that dealing with John had nearly depleted his coaching faculties. Still, the fans kept chanting John's name. They could be heard even when he wasn't on the ice.

After the incident in Montreal, John spent more time at Nancy's. He began staying there for longer periods of time. As a result of his increasingly irrational behavior, his relationship with Fogarty was suffering. Fogarty didn't approve of John's habit of frequenting those parts of Old Quebec known for its clandestine drug trade. John spent a lot of time on rue St-Paul where he partied at L'Acropole, a bar nestled among a row of trendy shops and restaurants. He knew several of the patrons and the bar's owner, Camille Page. Undercover officers were also in and out of the bar, keeping it under regular surveillance, as part of a Gendarme Royale du Canada effort known as Operation Chacal.

Pierre Page gave John the green light to practice with the team again. John's test results had been inconclusive. Page spoke with team doctors regarding the puzzling results. John's sample tested positive, but the lab technicians indicated they were not convinced the amounts were significant enough to establish that result fairly. There was also a question of exactly what substance appeared in John's urine. There was no clear indication of alcohol or drugs. Based on those findings, it was difficult to determine whether or not John actually failed the test. Page, though, credited John with the first breach of the drug-testing guidelines in his contract. John knew that a second one would mean automatic dismissal.

John was bigger than ever, 225 pounds of chiseled, rippled muscle mass. He easily had the finest physique in the NHL. Players either kidded him about looking in the mirror too much, or about missing his calling as a competitive body-builder. John slugged around dramatically heavy pound-ages in the Colisée weight room, or at a gym owned by Quebec bodybuilding superstar Bruce Cashman. (John was maxing out at 300 pounds and more in the bench press.) Cashman was well known in Canadian bodybuild-ing circles, and steadfastly rejected claims that he built his competition-level physique through steroids. His rebuttals were largely shrugged off by other bodybuilders, many Nordiques players, and John, who saw them as Cashman's way of holding on to his credibility.

It was obvious to anyone near John that he was taking steroids. He began by cycling his intake, grading the types of steroid taken, usually in six- to eight-week periods, then starting over again. He told Nancy he was following the regimen to peak his strength for the start of the hockey season. Now, halfway into it, he graduated to more exotic steroids, ones that made his size and strength improbable. He was told these substances would not make him sick. He was forced to inject them intramuscularly, into the fleshy lobe of his buttocks. The drugs would be eliminated by the body's normal functions if they were taken intrave-nously. It meant he had to use a large needle and syringe more common to veterinary practices. It was a painful pro-cedure. He hated the needle. At times, the needle broke off in his flesh. The effect, though, was undeniably evident.

•   •   •   •   •

By the beginning of 1992, Page was leaving John in Quebec more and more during road trips. After a while, the general manager decided to make it a permanent policy. John spent his downtime with Nancy. He told her he hated himself for hurting people. He was sullen when the team was away, spending a lot of his time watching the daytime soap opera "The Young and the Restless" on TV. During a scene when one of the characters was teetering over a bottle of vodka, Nancy heard him shout, "Go ahead and drink it."

There were some happy moments, too, usually when John was giving vent to his competitiveness in the gym.

But then he would return to his sessions in front of the television. His favorite song was The Crash Test Dummies' "Superman," and he asked for silence during Guns 'n' Roses "November Rain." The song's video often disturbed him. The video's climactic funeral scene turned his thoughts to his father, and he would cry. And it was as if his soul were fluttering just beneath the surface of his skin.

Nancy kept her house clean, and that meant cleaning up after John. Her sister, Marie-Pierre, was over a lot to see John. She could laugh with him, more so than with many of her friends, male or female. She also practiced speaking English with John. She once asked Nancy for something for a cold she was fighting. Nancy said she hadn't bothered to keep her medicine cabinet updated. Her sister remembered John kept cough syrup bottles in the upstairs washroom.

"Yes, it's grape flavor," Nancy said, opening the mirrored cabinet. She opened a bottle and brought it to her nose.

"Ahhh, it smells like shit, get it away from me."

"Oh, c'mon, cough syrup always smells bad, that doesn't mean it's not good."

"Fine, you try it then."

Marie-Pierre turned her head, jeering, a funny look on her face.

"Merde . . . what did he do, piss in them?"

Marie-Pierre was right. There were five cough syrup

bottles, each filled with urine. John laughed himself to the floor when he learned Marie-Pierre actually brought one to her mouth to taste its contents.

Page met with John's family as winter embraced Quebec. The Kordic family was concerned with the degree of help the Nordiques were providing for John. They also discussed John's paranoia with police. (They stressed that fact, as if urging Page to read the writing on the wall.)

Page strengthened his safety net around John. He had a sports psychologist from McGill University work with John. He also opened the door to a high-ranking police officer, with whom John could have off-record discussions. By this time, the press had figured out that a lot of John's problems were linked to drugs. Page continued to refuse to respond to any mention of drugs and John. When John was scratched from the lineup, he gave no reasons other than to say that John wasn't playing. He adopted the same strategy when asked if John had failed his first testing session. His convictions about the NHL drug policy were stronger than ever now, especially since his eyes, or his heart, couldn't follow John around all hours of the day.

The phone rang in Nancy's kitchen a couple of times before she could make her way from the living room to answer it.

It was John. She knew his voice at once. She had kept many of the messages John left on her answering machine. When she played them back, she could tell if he was high, or if he was straight, just by the sound of his voice.

John was in a bedroom at the Hotel Pierre, on Hamel Boulevard.

"I'm phoning to say goodbye."

"Why don't you say hi?" she answered.

"Because I've had enough . . . I took pills . . . I'm not going to see you anymore."

Nancy called Fogarty immediately, and asked him where John was. He balked at first. He knew John was high, and if one more drug-related incident came to light, his friend would be out of a career. When he realized this was a life-and-death situation, he told Nancy where John was.

A short while later, Nancy rushed into the Hotel Pierre and asked for the manager. Several police officers were on her heels. The manager could not be located, and the front-desk clerk couldn't find John's name on the registry.

She began pounding on doors, the police still behind her. Finally, they came to a door where no one answered. She realized at once that John could be inside. An officer lowered his shoulder, slamming into the door, and it flung open. Inside, John was propped up in bed, the covers pulled up to his abdomen. He looked startled, confused. He demanded to be left alone. There was a bottle of sleeping pills on the nightstand. He rejected police advice to go to the hospital, repeating that he wanted to be left alone.

Nancy managed to get John home, all the while trying to keep the atmosphere casual. But finally, she had to know: "John, why do you do this? So many people have tried to help you and you still do these things."

"I know what I am . . . I'm too far gone."

"It's not that way, I know you, and I know you are a good person."

"All my life I wanted to make my father proud . . . it's like I can feel him inside me. I don't know anymore, maybe if I was dead I'd be closer to him, maybe I deserve to be dead . . . My dad was my idol and when he died I was mad at myself. I never said the things I should have said. My whole career, I did it against his will."

"You are a hockey player, John, you made that happen, he was proud of you for that."

"I fought all the time, my coaches said one thing and my father said another, and I'm fucked between them . . . For a long time I've been thinking about this," he continued. "I'm not going to live to be his age. I'm not going to make it to 40."

Chapter Twenty-six

IN LATE JANUARY 1992, John's second test results were in: his sample contained significant traces of drugs and alcohol. There was no second-guessing this time.

Page met with his players to outline the situation. He told them John's problems would be placed in the hands of a clinical psychologist. He left the final verdict on John's future to a private-player vote. When the tally came in, there was no reprieve for John—he was voted off the team. The only duty Page had left was to tell him, face-to-face.

Once informed of the decision, John rushed to his own defense, insisting that there was something wrong with the tests.

"You can't do that, this is what I need, I have a chance to get better."

Page stood firm. Several days before, he had responded to yet another call from Fogarty. That time, he had sent John to stay with Nancy, and then changed the locks on Fogarty's doors.

"Your best chance is in a clinic now, John. You had a $150,000 bonus at end of year if you stayed clean and that wasn't enough motivation . . . you have to deal with this now. I've talked to other alcoholics and they said they got in fights and nearly died, that's what changed it around for them . . . you've got to come to a decision like that, you've got to do something about this or you could die."

John's release was made official on January 13, 1992. He appeared in 19 of the Nords' first 44 games, had two

assists, and amassed 115 penalty minutes. In his statements to the media, Page said, "We appreciate what John
did for the team, but we've decided to make a few changes
to alter the chemistry." Page gave no hint that drugs or
alcohol had prompted the hockey player's release. John's
response was less diplomatic: "Pierre Page said he got rid
of me for the good of the team's chemistry . . . well, if
that's the case, he's going to have to get rid of four or five
other players, as well." Page's only response was that John
"did not have the credibility to make such accusations."
John also told Nancy and his family that he wasn't the
only player on the team using drugs. He named four others
as recreational users. The names eventually leaked to reporters, but were never revealed in any of their stories.

Once more out of hockey, John settled into Nancy's
house permanently. He told her he was returning home to
Edmonton for a brief period. He had spoken to Edmonton
Oilers' general manager Glen Sather the previous summer.
Sather was well known and well respected among NHL
players for giving problem players a chance at redemption.
He had extended opportunities to Link Gaetz and Craig
MacTavish, the latter after a tragic drunk-driving mishap.
Within two weeks, John and Sather agreed to a contract
that would send John to the AHL's Cape Breton Oilers. Of
significance to John was his status as an NHL reserve
player. There were no provisions for drug or alcohol testing.

For the first time in a long time, he was cocky, full of
the attitude that had served him well when he was a junior. There were no more trips to L'Acropole, or to the
other bars he had frequented. Since his release from the
Nords, he was drinking very little. Most days, he didn't
touch alcohol. Instead, he devoutly primed his body at the
gym. Nancy understood John's enthusiasm. Throughout
his career, John had fought for ice time on a regular shift,
not a tap on the shoulder when the situation called for an
enforcer. Now, however, he wasn't fighting for it any
longer. Now, he concentrated on building his strength; the
kind of strength that would be noticed in the AHL, and by
Sather, who always respected the enforcer's role. He was

confident he could readily conquer all comers in the AHL. And if he succeeded, a call to the NHL wouldn't be far away. As he said to his friend, Raj Samarval, "I'm going to be awesome."

Before he left, John held Nancy's hand and told her he would write her every day, and phone every night. Now that he was going, he said, he wanted to consummate his feelings and try for a baby, when he returned. John left Quebec with a feeling of elation and relief.

A few of the Cape Breton Oilers were lounging at Cutters Bar when someone announced that John Kordic had arrived. It was John's first night in Cape Breton, and already he had been told by locals that Cutters Bar was a players' hangout. John immediately distinguished the players from the regular patrons. Louie DeBrusk shook his hand, and introduced him to Dan Curry, François Laurie, and some of the others. Drinks were a dollar each at Cutters. The bar ran its "looney night" once a week, which made it popular with everyone. When they were in the mood to party, the players hit looney night first, before ending the evening at Smooth Herman's.

John found out quickly that the team had a dress code: the leather jacket that Nancy had given him wouldn't do. He settled into the Holiday Inn later, rooming with DeBrusk, who loaned John a blazer.

Earlier that day, John had met his new coach, Don Mc-Adam, and general manager Dave Andrews, at Memorial Coliseum. Andrews was a year away from graduating to the league presidency. When Andrews introduced himself, John asked him if he was the same Dave Andrews who coached the Victoria Cougars ten years ago when he broke into junior hockey. Andrews acknowledged the fact. John said it was a small world, and that a lot of water had passed under the bridge since.

Most of the players were leery of John. They had learned about him from Scott Thornton, who had played briefly with the Leafs, alongside John. Whenever John asked if any of the players were going out for dinner, he would be met with excuses. After almost a week of rejections, he yelled out in the dressing room, "Doesn't anybody fuckin' eat around here?"

The Cape Breton Oilers played the Canadiens farm team from Fredericton in John's first game with the organization. Fredericton still carried Mario Roberge, who was considered one of the toughest scrappers in the league. John had fought Roberge back in the Canadiens' training camps. He didn't waste time reacquainting himself in Cape Breton. On his first shift, they met along the boards in a solid check. As they bounced off each other, their gloves dropped. John emerged triumphant to a wildly approving crowd. The players, noting that Roberge was bleeding from a cut over his eye, were impressed. They had never seen Roberge bleed before.

The Oilers went on a ten-game winning streak afterward. John was paired with Debrusk on what was the league's most rugged forward line. Most teams were wary of the duo, and played what was referred to as a "soft" game against the Oilers. John attained top billing at home and in visiting rinks. He prompted talk in the stands and in the media, especially after a bout with Adirondack tough guy Kirk Tomlinson at Glen Falls. They clashed twice in one game to settle a score. John always put on a show when he did battle, shedding his helmet and jersey, and madly peeling off his elbow pads. When he was done, referees kept both hands on him all the way to the penalty box. He swore at his foe or the officials from the penalty box, where he was a sweating, heaving mass, in varying stages of undress. His cursing often got him game misconducts. The players knew he sometimes talked himself out of games as a way of hiding the fact that he was exhausted. He usually had very little energy left after his bouts.

McAdam let John assume the unofficial role of team motivator. His in-your-face manner actually scared one European player. During one of his verbal scourings, Tomas

Srsen, a rookie draft choice from Czechoslovakia, bleated, "John, I have a wife and kids, please . . ."

John fed off the moments he gave to his teammates, who by now respected him while realizing the unpredictability of his moods. John often walked across the ice when a visiting team was in its morning skating routine before a game. He would wear his tight T-shirt, and eye his foes conspicuously, then say, "You can run, but you can't hide."

He heard a CBC radio interview with Richie Walcott, a hometown boy from Sydney, Nova Scotia. Walcott, a rookie with the Baltimore Skipjacks who had earned a reputation as an up-and-coming scrapper, was baited into talking about an inevitable bout with John. When the moment came, John was leaning over his stick at the face-off circle. "Let's go," he told Walcott. "We've got to go sometime, let's do it now. You've been shooting your mouth off, let's do it before they drop the puck." Walcott ignored John but had no choice once the puck was dropped. After an uneventful bout, they shouted insults at each other in the penalty box, which got them both thrown out of the game. In the dressing room, his uniform partly peeled off, John motioned for a security guard. "Hey, can you get Walcott for me?" Minutes later, Walcott was there, gaping at John's massive physique. John welcomed him in. All he wanted to do was share a few fighting tips with the rookie, share a few dos and don'ts in case the younger player graduated to the NHL one day. Afterward, during an interview, Walcott said what a gentleman John was and referred to him as "Mr. Kordic."

McAdam had arranged for John to room with DeBrusk. They had adjacent rooms at the Cape Breton Holiday Inn, and were roommates on road trips. At first, DeBrusk, a hulking 20-year-old who was the Ontario Hockey League's premiere enforcer in the late 1980s and early nineties, was not enamored of the arrangement. He would have preferred Thornton, one of his OHL buddies and a former Belleville Bull. DeBrusk, though, understood Mc-

Adam's thinking, and so did John. DeBrusk was a recovering alcoholic.

Hours before a road trip to Adirondack, McAdam was called to the Holiday Inn. He'd received word that DeBrusk had holed up in his room and wasn't opening the door to anyone. When he arrived, McAdam found the door locked. No amount of negotiating or reasoning seemed to have any effect. After a while, Andrews arrived at the hotel and joined the vigil outside the hockey player's door. He called John, hoping Kordic could reach DeBrusk. It was then that he saw a side to John he would never forget. Strong and compelling, John tried to reason with DeBrusk, to no avail. It was decided that Andrews would stay behind until the matter was resolved. DeBrusk eventually broke his self-imposed isolation. He, too, had seen sides of John that he knew would never be recorded by the media. He smiled whenever he remembered John in a snowball fight with children; John's antics brought wails of laughter from his teammates when he jumped on the luggage conveyor belt at the airport to find out what the holdup was with the team's baggage. Across the dressing room, DeBrusk often noticed John's introspection before games. John always had the opposing team's stats in his locker, was always talking to scouts and trainers. He wanted to know everything about who he might be squaring off against. DeBrusk remembered something the boxer Mike Tyson had once said about a hero and a coward being the same person, except that the coward walked away from a fight, a hero stayed. DeBrusk thought John Kordic was a hero.

DeBrusk rode in Andrews's car and arrived in Glens Falls in the second period. When they came through the arena doors, John was flailing away with Tomlinson in their second bout of the evening.

The Oilers were billed as an earnest Calder Cup contender until the first round of the play-offs. They faced the St. John's Maple Leafs, and after splitting the first two games on the road, they dropped the series. McAdam made a goaltending change in the first game back in Cape

Breton, a game which the Oilers went on to lose despite outshooting the Leafs by an almost two-to-one margin. Several players paraded into Andrews's office afterward to protest the move.

One day near the end of the season, DeBrusk saw John almost naked in their hotel room, holding a large syringe near his buttock. This wasn't a new occurrence; he had seen John giving himself injections in the past. John regularly performed the brief procedure within an hour or two of a game. Inside the syringe was a testosterone suspension, a common steroid suspended in water. Its effect was immediate, a chemical boost which, when taken in the water suspension, was voided by the body after exercise. DeBrusk had witnessed John's strength all season long. It was ironic that John had advised him against smoking and taking steroids, both of which John indulged in.

"John, what are you doing this for? Aren't you hurting yourself, buddy?"

John's answer: "I'm not afraid to die."

John mostly kept to himself, maintained his steroid cycling program, watched television, phoned Nancy, or called his agent to see if there was any word from Edmonton. In the two months he played with Cape Breton, no one ever came to him with a drug- or alcohol-related concern. However, when he was without a ride to the arena, he would hail a taxi, and in the back seat, give himself an injection of steroids. After the last game of the year, as the players were filing out of the dressing room, John was on the floor, pumping out his usual count of 200 to 300 push-ups.

Sather never did call John, or John's agent. In Edmonton, the Oilers, who had advanced to the conference final against the Chicago Blackhawks, had plenty of muscle in Dave Brown, who was taller and heavier than John, and every bit as nasty. Grandstanding for his teammates, and the press, John called Sather a liar. John told them he was ready and willing to do the job fans once chanted his name for. The players knew John's contract was without any concrete provision of a call-up to Edmonton. Still, the NHL was in a work stoppage as Cape

Breton faded from the AHL play-offs. John held a flicker of hope that when play resumed, he would be summoned to Edmonton.

With hockey over for the season, he decided to return to Quebec, to Nancy, and have some fun. He thought he wouldn't be hurting anyone that way.

Chapter Twenty-seven

WHEN JOHN came back to Quebec, Nancy told him she thought she was pregnant. He welcomed the news; Nancy, however, was not too happy about the prospect. She didn't want to have a baby until John had purged himself of his habits. When the test came back negative, John was disappointed, and she was relieved.

In June, John asked Nancy to marry him.

"I love you," John said, and gave her his promise of a life together.

When she saw the ring that he'd attached to a rose, she pulled John to her, as close as she could manage. After that moment, she never took the ring off.

"Don't tell anyone you ever saw me cry," John said, a tear trailing down his cheek.

By July 1992, John was spending much of his time in the gym. His cycling program, combined with lifting weights, bulked his muscle mass to more than 235 pounds. Although he was impressed with the results, his breathing was labored and his perspiration more extreme than ever.

John visited with family and friends during a brief trip to Edmonton. His brother, Danny, had been drafted by the Philadelphia Flyers. Danny had grown into a lanky, six-foot-four frame which John thought would make for good sibling rivalry when he made it back to the NHL with the Oilers.

John still owed too many people money to stay in one place for too long. He was being sought by people from Washington and New York. Back in Quebec, John had resurfaced at L'Acropole where he met a man with ties to the biker-gang drug culture. He drove John around: to bars, to connections, and especially to John's bank. In late July, John deposited his final NHL check, a $16,000 payment from the Nords, into a bank in St. Foy. Within days, he began to make regular withdrawals, hundreds of dollars at a time. Some withdrawals were as high as $2,000.

By the end of July, John was given to moods of violent paranoia. The drug he thought was an aphrodisiac eventually scuttled his sex life—which he placed above almost everything in his life. When Nancy resisted his advances, he grew increasingly hostile and jealous of her former boyfriend. In his rages, he accused Nancy of infidelity. One night, Nancy's former boyfriend called her from a bar. He was drunk. Hearing John yelling over her voice, he insisted on coming over. John immediately came on the line and threatened him, telling the man to stick to his wife and children. Within a half hour, Nancy's former boyfriend was at the front door. An argument ensued, with Nancy holding John back until the incident was over. By that time, most of the neighborhood was aware of the yelling and swearing. Seconds later, several police cruisers screeched to a halt in front of the house.

A file picture of John appeared in the papers the next day, along with a story of his arrest and the news that he had been served with a restraining order. Nancy pleaded to have the charges dropped, saying she merely wanted John out of the house. Her protests, though, had no effect on the police. It was the third domestic call they had received for her address.

John was released from police custody on his own recognizance, with a court date set for August 11. For the next ten days, he was forbidden to have contact with his fiancée. He was also without a place to live.

John looked at his bank account before making a call to Minnesota. He contacted Dr. Fearing, who had left Hazelden and established his own sports psychology service, which he ran with former Canadiens great Bobby

Smith. John arranged for Fearing to arrive in Quebec the day before his court appearance. He had enough money to pay for Fearing's expenses, and made the offer to reimburse him upon arrival. John knew he was slipping. Page had told him something about how other problem players had "hit a wall" before they took steps towards recovery.

He'd stepped out on his own. It was hard to tell the difference between his pleasure and his pain anymore.

Chapter Twenty-eight

IT'S AUGUST 8, 1992, just after 3:00 a.m., and John orders a taxi to pick him up at the Motel Maxim.

John drops into the back seat of the cab. The driver recognizes him—Kordique, who played with Les Nordiques. It's less than six hours since he let John out at the hotel from a previous fare. John gives no directions. He says he just wants to drive around St. Foy. His words aren't coherent until he orders the man to stop at a convenience store. He returns with a pack of cigarettes and a large bottle of Pepsi, which he gulps down quickly. The cab roams around the Colisée, then back onto the Boulevard Capital. The driver tells John he has to turn the cab over for the day shift. He wants to meet another driver in an underground parking lot, but John orders him to stay on the street, above ground. Another corner store, and another pack of cigarettes. Just after four o'clock, John takes the driver's advice and changes cabs. Minutes later, the first driver finds two packs of cigarettes and a bank book where John was sitting. The bank book is from a checking account, the Laurentian Bank, St. Foy. It shows John deposited $16,000 from the NHL on July 24. The book showed a balance of $5,000.

"Take me to Mesnil," John tells the second driver, referring to a new housing development in the city's north end. He complains about the heat; the heater in the cab is not on. John cannot locate the house he wants in Mesnil. He stops for a bottled water, gulps half of it. The other half he spills in the back seat of the cab.

He tells the cabdriver to take him to 315 Boulevard Champlain. It's 5:00 a.m., and when he gets there, John disappears briefly into an apartment block. He comes out with Richard Blaine, a large, blond man with a potbelly. Blaine has been John's friend for six months. John's room at the Maxim was leased under Blaine's name the night before. John follows him to a car where the man gives him a blue Nordiques duffel bag.

The cab pulls into the lobby area of the Hotel Luxembourg on John's order. John flips a fifty-dollar bill at the receptionist. He doesn't want the change, but gets it anyway, along with a key.

After 6:00 a.m., he is phoning down to the front desk every 15 minutes, swearing, asking how the television set works.

At 7:00 a.m., he is out in the corridor again, but ducks back into his room.

After 8:00 a.m., he goes down to the front desk. The daytime receptionist recognizes him. He gives his key back and calls a taxi.

In the back of the cab now, breathing heavily. Deep breaths and confusion.

"Fuck . . . it hurts." The driver sees John is hitting his head with his fists. The cab stops at a corner store and John buys a bottle of Coke. John wants to go back to the Luxembourg.

In the hotel lobby now, John leans heavily against the counter. His breathing is labored and he has trouble standing. He stammers as he asks for the room he had just a few hours ago. The woman tells him it's not available. He takes another room and leaves the counter without paying because he has no money in his pockets.

At 10:00 a.m., he's on the phone. Repeated calls now. He asks "Where am I?" then "Who are you?"

At noon, Blaine picks him up and drives him to Laurentian Bank. John slams the door shut and returns in minutes. He has made a $1,000 withdrawal.

Back in his hotel room. It is just past 3:00 p.m. when he asks the front desk to have six beers delivered to his room.

A few minutes later, John tries to reach for the delivery through the opening between the door and the chain latch, but his hand is too large to pass through. Finally, he pulls the door open wide enough to take the six pack from the hotel employee. His foot is blocking the door from opening entirely.

There is blood on his hands, blood in the room. He is wrapped in a towel stained with his blood. Seconds after the door closes, there is the sound of bottles crashing and breaking in his room.

Three patrons entering the hotel see John at his door. When they walk by his window, they see blood on the pane. One of them recognizes him as the Nordiques hockey player and returns to the front desk.

"This guy is going to die," she says.

Just after 5:00 p.m., John leaves the Luxembourg in a taxi. In his hotel room, there is a hole in the ceiling, and a mirror broken on the floor near a chair, which is also broken. A discarded razor is on the floor, and all around the room there is blood—on the carpet, sheets, mattress, walls, window, curtains, dresser, closet. No one discovers the chaos until the following morning when the maids enter the room to clean it.

It is near 6:00 p.m. John goes back to the Maxim.

"Salut, John," says Madelaine Bouchard, who is working the front desk at the Maxim. He doesn't answer.

"Are you sure you are okay? You should go to a hospital."

"I just wanna sleep."

John sees Serge Bouchard, the hotel's director, and asks him where room 205 is. He drops his bags as soon as he gets into the room, then phones to arrange a wake-up call for 11:00 p.m.

Just after 9:00 p.m., John is on the phone to Serge Bouchard: "What the fuck's going on? Where am I right now?" John hangs up and calls back, repeatedly, saying things that don't make sense.

Madelaine takes over at the desk. John is still calling. "John, do you need some help?" she asks.

"Fuck off . . . Who the fuck are you?"

At 10:03 p.m., Serge Bouchard phones the L'Ancienne Lorette police station.

"I have a problem with one of my clients, John Kordic . . . He's in one of my rooms, and he's having a bad trip, a really bad one, okay?"

The officer who is working dispatch calls Sergeant Alain Poulain, who is on the road in his cruiser.

"I have a good job for you. You have to go to the Maxim Motel, go by reception. It's for John Kordic in room 205. He's having a bad trip."

John is in his room, in his own private hell. He's breathing heavily, his face is enlarged, puffy, red. There is a pounding in the veins in his eyes, neck, forehead. They are abnormally pronounced. He is covered in a hot sweat. He is extremely paranoid. The only person he is a danger to at the moment is himself.

At 10:09 p.m., two other officers radio Poulain.

"We'll meet there, Alain?"

"Yes, yes, we'll meet at the Maxim. We'll go see the owner, find out what's going on, and then we'll decide what technique to use."

"If worst comes to worst, if we have to hold him down and all that, maybe we better call the [ambulance] people and do that all together in a gang . . . if we have to, to arrest him or stop him."

"Yeah, I know," the officer replied. "I'll go and see the owner, we'll talk to him before, then we'll see what kind of guy this is and how we will react. I don't think he's a guy who will give trouble to the police."

It is 10:30 p.m. Poulain and the two officers are in the lobby and near enough to hear John's calls ringing through to the front desk.

"John, there is an ambulance here. Would you like to get help from them?" Serge Bouchard says into the receiver.

Serge's father, Martin, tells the officers that John is very strong. Maybe they will not be able to restrain him, he says.

Martin Bouchard asks his son to phone Nancy, then Blaine, known acquaintances of John who may be able to help. Serge tries to contact them, but neither can be located.

Martin Bouchard then suggests that his son and employee Yvon Brassard, who know John well, go to the room to speak with him. The police will be in the stairway to intervene if necessary.

John hears a knock at his door. He comes to answer it, his condition obvious, and lets the two men in. The room is a mess. A chair is turned over on the floor, curtain rods are dangling and picture frames are broken. John's blood is on the bed sheets.

"What did you do to the room?" Serge asks.

John mutters something. He is wearing Bermuda shorts, and a cutoff T-shirt. There are lines on his cheeks, like scratches.

"Fuck . . . I don't fuckin' know . . . it's all fucked."

His hands are clenched hard into fists, and he hits his chest repeatedly. He paces the room. All the while, Serge explains that people do not want to hurt him, they only want him to leave. If he doesn't comply, Serge tells him, the police will evict him.

In the hallway, patrons can hear John yelling that he doesn't want to go to jail. After another altercation with John, Serge leaves the room.

Bouchard bends to gather John's clothing.

"What are you doing . . . you're trying to plant fuckin' drugs in my stuff."

John's hands grind into his pocket and come up with $50 bills. He throws them on the floor before Bouchard.

"John, here, have a cigarette."

"Sure, it's got drugs in it too." He throws it to the floor.

As it lands, Bouchard looks away, towards the door. He reaches it in a few steps, then outside into the hallway where the police were waiting.

Serge asks the police to take over. He warns them that three police officers would not be able to handle John. He also suggests that they tell John the police do not intend to press charges.

Two police officers inside the room, and John, on his feet, restlessly moves around inside a small space by his bed. Bouchard tries again to put John's clothing into his bags.

"He put stuff in my bag," John shouts to the officers.

An officer tells John they are there to discuss the situation with him. The officer is not bilingual. He speaks a broken English.

It's 10:37 p.m., and Poulain calls the Sûreté de Québec (Quebec Provincial Police) for assistance. Less than two minutes later, the QPP dispatcher is on the radio. He briefs two officers cruising the Boulevard Hamel near Filion.

"The 51 is there, at the Hotel Maxim . . . It's gonna take big arms."

At 10:43 p.m., two QPP cruisers rush to the scene, lights flashing.

"The Kordic case is not a surprise," one says over the radio. "He's going to finish by killing himself, that son of a bitch."

Poulain orders all officers to remove their weapons before entering the room.

In the room, Poulain orders his officer to execute the arrest, for disorder and mischief, and instructs him to read the Miranda. Poulain does not speak English when he gives his order.

Poulain thinks he sees John spit at his officer.

To the officers, now, John is out of control. There are seven uniforms in or near the room.

John strides to the opposite end of the room, next to the patio window. He turns to them, and draws in deep breaths, as if to pump up his chest. He drops into the rushing stance of a football player, then charges into them, bulling to the door. Their first reaction is to grab John's arms, one officer on each arm. They are both lifted into the air. They cannot stop him. One hits a wall, and the other slams into the television set.

A policewoman clutches John's leg, and another officer pushes forward into John's shoulder.

His balance failing, John careens to his knees, then onto his left side. He has two officers on top of him, and as they struggle to regain control, he is sent over onto his stomach. He tries to get up, but an officer has one knee between John's shoulder blades, driving his weight downward.

Three other officers are around him, holding down his head, his shoulders, and legs. They shout at one another as their attempts to cuff John's arms fail. They manage to cuff both his wrists individually, then bind the cuffs behind his back with a third set of cuffs.

John raises his head. One of the officers sees there is blood and a bubbled, white, saliva-like fluid gurgling from his mouth. This is the first sign of cardiac arrest.

"He's soiling the carpet," Martin Bouchard shouts from the hallway. The hotel owner hands the policewoman a towel. She uses it to swab John's mouth.

At 10:46 p.m., Poulain calls the Quebec City ambulance service.

At 10:51 p.m., officers in two more QPP cruisers hear the radio talk from the Maxim, and book on to the detail. Inside one of the QPP cruisers is Sergeant Janvier, who is aspiring to be a staff sergeant. They bring a four-foot section of rope up to room 205. There are now seven QPP officers in the room, along with the three from L'Ancienne Lorette.

At 10:52 p.m., the QPP dispatcher is told the situation at the Maxim is under control. Moments later, Brassard hears an officer yell out an order:

"Stop . . . he's black."

Brassard sees the officer lift his knee from between John's shoulder blades. Then there is another order:

"Okay, he's coming back . . . Give it back to him one more time." Brassard would be the only person in the room to remember hearing the second order.

A patron in the hallway looks into the room and recognizes John. He sees John's face clearly; it is red, an improbable red. Patches of skin on his cheekbones show the network of veins beneath. John's mouth is half-open, his tongue partly protruding, and a bubbly froth is oozing from between his lips.

"Make some air for him," Martin Bouchard says, speaking into the doorway.

No one listens to him. Instead, John is told he is under arrest and has the right to consult a lawyer.

Ambulance attendants finally arrive. The stretcher is too large to fit through the door, and there is barely

enough space around the police to get through the doorway.

Ambulance attendant Mario Desrosiers is nearing the
doorway when he sees a man who says, "Pick that up, that
garbage, and get it out of my hotel." He sees John's face,
the officers still pinning him to the ground, and asks if
everything is okay. There is no answer.

Poulain presses his finger into John's reddened cheek.
He releases, and when he sees the white of the depression
turn red again, he concludes that John's circulation is satis-
factory.

As the stretcher is folded and brought into the room,
Desrosiers is nudged aside, along the wall, to make room.
As he is moved, he sees QPP sergeant Janvier standing on
John's body. There is a slight grin on the sergeant's face, as
if he has bagged a hunting trophy. Desrosiers will be the
only one to remember this detail.

John is pushed and prodded until he is on the stretcher.
His body stiffens. He does not make a sound.

Desrosiers registers John's pulse and performs a capil-
lary test on his finger. The indication is that John's circulation is normal. He then feels for a pulse on his neck.

Martin Bouchard, like the others in the hallway,
watches in silence. He sees John's color is a ghastly blue.
He drifts away from the scene, goes to the lobby where he
sees Yvon Brassard.

"I think John Kordic is dead," he says.

Brassard looks on, unnerved, horrified. He will not
sleep for nights while his mind replays the nightmares he
has seen.

Police secure John to the stretcher with five straps. The
four-foot section of rope is knotted around his ankles, and
the cuffs are not removed. John is facedown, on his stomach. All through the binding procedure, he doesn't move.

Through the hallway now. John is taken down the
stairs head first. To the police and ambulance attendants,
this passes for normal procedure—to have the pressure of
John's bulk focused on his thorax area, where, inside, his
lungs are fighting for air.

Dominique D'Arveaux, a nurse at the University of
Sherbrooke Hospital, stands in the doorway of her room

at the Maxim as the stretcher is carried down the hall. She has seen John's condition mirrored in other patients. In medical terms, it is referred to as "cyanized, marbled, pulped." She recognizes that John's body is in a state of muscular stiffness.

Back at room 205, Martin Bouchard points to the bloodstains on the carpet. Sergeant Janvier is standing near him. He tells the policeman he will pay for the cleaning bill by subtracting the costs from the money John previously tossed onto the floor. Janvier had gathered the bills, totaling $125, and placed them on a table in the room. He objects to Bouchard's suggestion. He locks the door and tells Bouchard not to enter unless authorized by a L'Ancienne Lorette officer.

In the ambulance now, the doors close behind a police officer who must ride along since John is under arrest. A check seconds ago, when the stretcher was being moved down the stairs, showed John's pulse to be all right.

As the ambulance makes a turn onto Boulevard Hamel, Desrosiers reaches for John's wrist. There is no pulse.

Just as the ambulance passes the front lobby of the motel, the officer orders the driver to stop. He opens the side door and walks into the lobby to speak with another officer. He returns minutes later. It is 11:04 p.m.

Desrosiers loosens the straps on the stretcher. The ambulance rushes, lights flashing, towards the University Hospital du Laval. The attendant fixes a stethoscope to John's chest. Desrosiers moves it quickly, inches one way, then another. There is no sound.

"It's not going well," he says, looking at the officer.

They remove the handcuffs, turning John over onto his back. They check for a pulse, listen close to the mouth for breathing. John's pulse and respiration are gone.

Desrosiers lifts John's eyelids. The pupils are fixed, they do not react to light.

"Code 99!" he shouts. Cardiac arrest.

Hands now, massaging John's chest, and others, reaching for the oxygen balloon, fixing it around his mouth.

It is the rhythm of ignorance, John being given oxygen almost 20 minutes after the first sign of the onset of a cardiac arrest. It takes roughly 20 minutes for the brain to die in an oxygen-deprived state. They are giving oxygen to a dead man.

At the hospital in seven minutes, and the blur of a rolling stretcher and a medical team's reanimation efforts. It is 11:11 p.m.

At 11:41, Dr. Deschaine and his team stop their efforts to revive John. John Kordic is pronounced dead.

PART THREE

*The aftermath, the inquest, and
one unanswered question*

Chapter Twenty-nine

AS THE MEDICAL team hovered over John in the reanimation room at the University Hospital du Laval, L'Ancienne Lorette police were gathering his personal effects from his motel room. It was police procedure to attempt to locate any medication that could alert doctors to a possible antidote.

Every item in the room was photographed: the bloodstains on the carpet, and evidence of struggle and damage to the room.

Along with John's clothes and bags, there were three used syringes taken from room 205. There was also a box of syringes, an empty bottle of Sten (a blend of three steroids manufactured in Mexico), and bottles containing more common steroids: Muscle Flex, Unitess Suspension, Boldone, and Winstrol V. John had also been carrying his grade six Bible.

At 1:00 p.m. August 9, 1992, an autopsy presided over by Dr. George Miller was performed on John's body. He was measured at 1.88 meters and weighed at 96.5 kilograms. Miller reported that there were no bruises or lesions that were the result of a punch to the body.

Miller did record numerous scrapes and markings, which were classified as "rubbing injuries." John's spleen, which was weighed at 240 grams, was double normal weight. His liver, too, was found to be excessively heavy at 2,630 grams (a condition compatible with the intake of anabolic steroids). His lungs were also enlarged, more than three times the normal weight.

On August 12, Miller sent several biological specimens taken from John's body to a federal laboratory in Montreal, where toxicologist Christiane Ayotte would perform blood and urine analyses.

On August 13, a clerk with the Quebec ambulance services in Quebec City mailed an invoice to Nancy's residence, which was also John's last mailing address. The invoice broke down the costs of transporting John from the Maxim to the hospital. There was a flat rate of $100, plus a charge for the seven kilometers covered by the ambulance, at $1.75 per kilometer.

The amount owed came to $112.25.

John's body was flown back to Edmonton. Nancy went to Edmonton to be with John's family. He was to be remembered in a funeral service at the Croatian church and buried at St. Albert's Cemetery, next to the plot where his father was laid to rest almost three years earlier. Father Cunningham read the service before some 400 people.

In the days and weeks following John's death, the Kordic family endured immeasurable pain. Much of it stemmed from portrayals in the media of John as a goon, portrayals which speculated about his private and family life.

In total, there would be over 500 stories written about John's demise, which were carried in hundreds of papers across North America.

Much of the coverage linked John's on-ice troubles to his well-documented alcohol dependency. *Sports Illustrated* came the closest to defining the reality of John's troubles. In an *SI* profile entitled "Death of a Goon," Bruce Cashman, who roomed with John during the summer of 1992 in Quebec City, declared that "John wasn't an alcoholic . . . He drank, yes, but only when he was doing drugs. He was a drug addict. He was addicted to cocaine, had been since he played for Montreal. He said it was a big thing on the Canadiens." Cashman also recounted a conversation in which John said coaches in

Montreal were aware that some players, including team stars, were snorting cocaine: "John said a coach walked into a hotel room where a couple of players were doing drugs . . . and the coach just said, 'I didn't see that,' turned around, and walked out the door." The story, published in the August 24 issue, also damned the NHL for flipping "the switch that turned on this fighting machine, but [not having] a clue about how to turn it off."

Predictably, reporters from every major newspaper in Canada and the United States converged on the Kordic household. They were present when Regina cried at John's grave site, and as she laid three blue candles on the freshly turned earth.

On August 12, John's sister, Lillian Kordic, wrote a letter on behalf of her family, a letter that was published shortly afterward in an Edmonton newspaper.

In part, it read: "Over the course of the last few days, we have sat back, watched, heard, and read my brother's character being besmirched. It is not an enviable position for those who loved him, for we, too, have not been spared. Our family's grief, agony, and suffering is apparently considered newsworthy enough for public consumption. To compound the issue, statements that are completely untrue have been made by those who obviously considered themselves to be informed . . . As a family, we feel now that he is gone, he should finally be left in peace. The chronology of his life via media exposure is unnecessary, for that which is represented is only a minuscule proportion of it."

On August 24, the same day of the *Sports Illustrated* story, an equally topical and far more controversial piece was published in the *Western Report*, a weekly magazine serving western Canada.

The magazine ran a picture of John on the front cover, with the headline "Death of An Enforcer." John was shown in the Canadiens dressing room, in a long-sleeved undershirt and track pants, sitting, his right leg bent and raised so his foot was resting on a bench. His left leg, relaxed, was at floor level. He was reaching around his knee to grab his right toes while his left hand was resting on his left thigh, pointed to the camera to show his bloodied and scarred knuckles.

The magazine quoted Bill Laforge, who had instructed John at the Tomahawk Hockey School in 1982. He was managing the Edmonton Huskies, a local semipro football team, and was also representing several NHL players. Laforge created a tempest in the WHL with his accounts of how the Winterhawks had set John upon a path of fighting and steroid use. Says Laforge:

"He told me that Shaw and Hodge said the only way he was going to the NHL was to fight, and to do that he had to be big. He started the steroids in his first year in juniors. He didn't want to fight, and didn't like doing it, but he was convinced he had to. They were the bosses—and they said fight."

Shaw dismissed Laforge's comments as the rantings of a spiteful former coach. Shaw recalled the WHL divisional final when Laforge accused the Hawks of feeding players performance-enhancing drugs.

"It's sour grapes. When he lost that game, he said the entire team took drugs in the second intermission, and that's why we won. His record shows just how much he knows about hockey . . ."

Shaw said that John was a "talented player who knew his role," and added that John tested clean under the team's mandatory drug-testing program.

"That's complete bull," Laforge countered. "If they tested him, it was to make sure he was taking enough drugs."

Shortly after the story ran, the magazine was contacted by the WHL's lawyer, who asked that they print a retraction and send a letter of apology to the league and the Winterhawks.

At the same time, Laforge, who had been a pallbearer at John's funeral, received a thank-you letter from Lillian:

"Thank you for your sympathy and condolences, but I really wanted to thank you for taking the time to talk to the [Western Report] writer. I read the article and truth be told it was one of the only ones I have any use for. I'm not saying it wasn't difficult, the cover itself perhaps was the worst part. You have hit closer to the truth than countless others, which is a great travesty in terms of commenting on our system. The truth hurts and it's quite ugly, and I know that down the road it is going to get a hell of a lot uglier."

On September 25, Dr. Miller completed the written report on the postmortem. John's cause of death was listed as: arrhythmic cardiac arrest followed by violent effort under the influence of cocaine, severe pulmonary edema, and aspirations of bronchitis and food substances in the lungs.

The sensationalism generated by John's death cooled across Canada as September wore on. There had been sufficient feature-length copy exploring the tragic life of a well-known hockey player gone wrong. The drugs, the fighting, the rumors made for intriguing gossip. The story died, though, once every lead and angle had been exhausted, and the police had nothing further to say.

But in Quebec City, there was renewed journalistic interest in probing the circumstances of John's death. The focus fell squarely on chief coroner Jean Grenier, with whom the decision lay to order public inquiries into deaths under police intervention and custody. An internal report was also being prepared by the QPP on the action of the arresting officers. On the airwaves, talk-show host Andres Arturs boldly suggested that the number of police officers in the room alone was enough to make one suspect police brutality. Jean Perron, John's former coach, ran his own popular talk show in Quebec City, and began stoking the story, as well.

Grenier now presided over a controversy that had gained momentum on the airwaves and in the minds of listeners and hockey fans. No amount of toxicological or pathological reports, or internal police reviews, would suffice.

Despite the evidence of John's cocaine and steroid use, one question still begged to be answered: Did police intervention cause John's death?

Chapter Thirty

GIL STEIN was president of the NHL at the time of John's death.

In the days after Kordic's death, under intense media scrutiny, he was called on many times to defend the effectiveness of the league's zero-tolerance drug policy. On one occasion, he went so far as to call it "draconian."

Stein staunchly asserted that the NHL was no place for drug users, and on that premise, he saw the policy as the best deterrent against drug use.

His "draconian" quip, though, bemused critics in the media and some player agents, who regarded him as somewhat Machiavellian (he had attempted to have himself elected to the Hockey Hall of Fame).

Stein, however, arranged to host a forum on August 31 in Toronto to discuss the league's drug policy. It was no coincidence that the event was scheduled at that time, so soon after John's death.

Stein invited parents of Toronto-area players drafted into the NHL in 1991 and 1992 to join a panel that included Martin Shain, of the Addiction Research Foundation (ARF), Mark Taylor, president of the ARF, and Patrick Ducharme, a Windsor-based criminal lawyer and legal representative for Bob Probert, who had called Stein and Ziegler dinosaurs and Neanderthals when asked for his comments on the NHL drug policy.

Among the parents who attended was Darryl Sittler, the former Leaf great whose son, Ryan, was a draft choice of the Philadelphia Flyers, which had also drafted John's brother, Dan.

The drug policy was widely criticized for leaving players with no option of coming forward with a problem. There was a consensus stemming from that criticism that John's problems might have been remedied long ago if there wasn't an overriding threat of a lifetime suspension.

Most people who knew John were deeply saddened by his death. The same people, however, players included, felt that John had been on a short track to self-destruction.

Many journalists began to wonder if the NHL would finally take John's death as a wake-up call. It was especially ironic, after Stein's remarks, that the NHL remained the only major professional sports league in North America without a comprehensive drug policy.

The league's apparent indifference is partly illustrated by their ignorance of Dr. Fearing's efforts to help John. After John's death, Fearing informed the NHL of his involvement with John. Neither O'Neil nor NHL director of hockey operations Brian Burke had any previous knowledge of this. Fearing requested return calls, but waited for months before he was contacted. Eventually, he became a member of a team of consultants hired by the league to develop a comprehensive drug policy.

Fearing also contacted NHL Players' Association (NHLPA) executive director Bob Goodenow. Goodenow expressed genuine interest in what Fearing knew about John's tragedy. He was also receptive to Fearing's suggestions about preventative strategies for the future.

Goodenow was the first significant power broker in the NHL to call for the league and its players' union to develop a drug policy.

"The bull has to be taken by the horns, and something has to be put into place," he told reporters. "Who's to say whether a comprehensive program would have helped John Kordic? But it certainly wouldn't have hurt."

Stein, who was not convinced that John had a drug problem, had announced that league officials would be pushing for a drug-testing policy as a measure of combating steroid use among players. He thereby reopened the issue of player drug tests. This issue had previously been raised during the 1986 Stanley Cup, when John was helping the Canadiens to a 4–2 series win over the Calgary Flames.

On May 21, 1986, between games three and four in Montreal, John Ziegler and Allan Eagleson, then executive director of the players' union, had announced a drug-testing proposal. Their proposal was in direct response to another controversial *Sports Illustrated* story of May 12 of that year, which exposed alleged drug problems among at least five players of the two-time Stanley Cup champion Edmonton Oilers.

In the *Sports Illustrated* story, three unnamed sources said they witnessed Oilers' players using cocaine at parties in Edmonton and other NHL cities. A non-Oiler player was also quoted as admitting that he had used cocaine with three Oilers in the previous season. And an agent said his Oilers' client told him, "Every time we go to New York City, it's a real blizzard and I'm not talking about the weather."

The chief of the RCMP's Edmonton drug squad was also quoted as saying, "We have information that there are users on the club"—a quote he later said was taken out of context.

When confronted with naming the players, *Sports Illustrated* editor Mark Mulvoy said the magazine did not have the names. He also indicated that the magazine did not publish supportive evidence out of fear of lawsuits.

The *Hockey News*, considered hockey's Bible, responded to the story by running a cover picture of simulated drug paraphernalia over an Oiler logo.

Ziegler and Eagleson, joined by Oilers coach and general manager Glen Sather, condemned both *Sports Illustrated* and the *Hockey News,* and declared both publications were guilty of "McCarthyism."

Ziegler and Eagleson's joint 1986 proposal called for:

- mandatory drug testing in the NHL;
- expansion of the NHL and NHLPA drug-education programs;
- continued strict adherence to the then current NHL drug policy of a lifetime suspension, not rehabilita-

tion, for any NHL player found to have used illegal drugs.

Although a vast majority of players insisted that the NHL did not have a drug problem, they balked at the prospect of drug testing.

Brian Trottier, then the New York Islanders captain and president of the NHLPA, said, "I know why Alan Eagleson and John Ziegler [proposed testing] . . . It's the same as Glen Sather wanting to do it to prove innocence. But players don't have to prove their innocence. They may want to, but they don't have to."

Oilers defenseman Randy Gregg, who graduated with a doctorate degree from the University of Alberta, had equally strong convictions. "This isn't child's play, this is very serious. I take this as an affront . . . Talk of urinalysis is so ludicrous. My feelings are, I have nothing to clear. If the caretaker or the person who cleans my street is willing to do a urinalysis, then I'm willing."

Where the issue of testing was concerned, the NHL and its players' union were like the immovable object meeting the irresistible force.

In his opening statements to the assembled parents, Stein acknowledged that the forum was "sparked by a conversation with a reporter after the death of John Kordic." He went on to say that it was his intention to open up discussion on the league's drug policy, as well as to invite the parents to participate with the panelists.

About 40 parents sat before the panelists in a cavernous conference room designed to hold several hundred people. An NHL banner was draped on the front wall, and klieg lights from a television studio were used to enhance illumination. The parents wore plastic name tags that were filled out by Dave Keon Jr., who was part of the sign-in staff.

"We're concerned about being tough and setting the rules up front," Stein said. "Our program is designed to deter players from ever trying drugs in the first place. It's not designed to help players who have become addicts. The emphasis is on deterrence . . . Other programs are based on the assumption that players are involved and they need help."

The parents were given a glossy file folder that contained the panelists' curricula vitae and summaries of drug policies from other hockey leagues, as well as from professional baseball, football, and basketball. (For the complete text of the respective drug policies of each league, see Appendix.) The parents were also given excerpts of Ziegler's decisions regarding the five players mentioned in the 1986 *Sports Illustrated* article.

Martin Shain declared that baseball had the best developed program for a professional athlete.

"Ideally, people should be able to seek assistance when personal problems threaten to hurt job performance," he said.

In his address to the parents, Patrick Ducharme expounded upon his strong convictions against the current policy.

"The hallmark of addictive behavior is denial," he said. "Kordic admitted he was an alcoholic, but he didn't dare say he was a drug addict . . . he couldn't do that.

"This is not a policy at all, it's simply a 'ban.' In my opinion it is arrogant in its indifference to a complicated problem.

"Drugs and alcohol are inextricably bound—we cannot separate the two.

"What an odd thing to talk about. If my son were entering the NHL, this is the last thing I'd want to hear about. You may be saying no way, not my son, he's a good boy, but you may be dead wrong. The kids are tailor-made prey for the downfall of addictive behavior.

"Think about the pressure they experience. They have to behave. They have to score. And there's always someone ready to take their place. They always have that hanging over their heads.

"To me, this lack of policy is crass in its nature. It ignores 50 years of intelligent research. It doesn't help the problem of denial, it makes it worse.

"I thought something really tragic would have to happen to drive the importance of this issue home."

Stein attempted to ingratiate himself to the audience by explaining his background as a former criminal lawyer. His oration included his memory of a case in which a budding star athlete killed a woman while stealing from her to support a drug habit.

"I can't believe it when I hear people describe these drugs in 'recreational' terms . . . they are destructive," he said.

"I don't accept Patrick Ducharme's viewpoint, that because they're [young players] going to the NHL, because they live in a big city and are under stress, they're going to turn to drugs.

"I don't agree with a policy of permissiveness."

Stein was alone in his remonstration. Several parents criticized the league's apparent distance from a comprehensive employee contract. They asked what the league held in higher value, its players, or its image.

Mark Taylor provided statistics about drug use in society. According to the Addiction Research Foundation, 80 percent of all people have used alcohol; 20 percent have tried illicit drugs. The rate of drug use in normal society and among professional hockey players was compared. There were no clear suggestions that hockey players mirrored societal habits on an equal ratio. It was considered, though, that hockey wasn't immune to society's problems. With that in mind, Taylor also said ARF statistics showed 60 percent of all North American companies with more than 500 employees have fundamental employee-assistance programs.

Darryl Sittler rose to voice his opinions. It was clear that he shared Ducharme's discontent with how the league dealt with potential drug problems in its players. He cited his own experiences as a star with the Leafs during the seventies. At that time, there was a plan under which players could see counselors, he said. The players, though, were constantly afraid that if management was privy to that information, it would be used against them in future contract negotiations. Sittler was also concerned about the prospect of his own son coming into contact with drugs.

"I agree with Patrick," Sittler said. "The Red Wings

knew about Probert's drug use before he got stopped at the border.

"We are role models, and we are susceptible to problems in our lives. It's too bad John Kordic had to die to make us have this meeting."

Chapter Thirty-one

ON SEPTEMBER 30, 1993, the book was literally closed on John's death with the release of a coroner's report in Quebec.

Coroner Gerald Locas, a judge and former schoolteacher from St. Hyacinthe, Quebec, wrote the 100-page document based on a public inquiry into the tragedy. It stood as the public record of how John died, and the role of all those involved during his final 24 hours.

Locas was entrusted with presiding over the inquest by Chief Coroner Jean Grenier. He concluded that John had died as the result of a lethal amount of cocaine in his system.

John met with sufficient physical force during the police intervention to promote the process, Locas wrote, although the police action and the ambulance personnel response was justified based on the methods presented to them during their training, and given John's resistance.

The inquest began October 7, 1992, and ended on April 26, 1993, after 39 days of hearings spread over seven months. Testimony was heard from 58 witnesses and two experts, and 61 items were introduced as evidence.

The Kordic family believed that John died in the hotel room. They were represented by lawyer Paul Bouchard of Sherbrooke, Quebec. Legal representation was also secured by the ambulance technicians, the municipality of L'Ancienne Lorette, the L'Ancienne Lorette police force, the City of Quebec, the Sûreté du Quebec, and the Canadian Centre for Drug-Free Sport.

Lawyers from the Montreal Canadiens and Quebec Nordiques were there during the proceedings, but did not seek official status. They appeared when Nancy was due to testify about the other NHL players who used cocaine, this based on stories told to her by John.

Nancy's testimony would have seriously jeopardized the careers of five Nordiques players. It would have generated a messy media campaign that would have made the fallout from the *Sports Illustrated* story of 1986 look tame. Moreover, it would have set a monumental precedent in professional team sports: never before had players been subpoenaed to a public inquiry into drug use in their sport.

When Nancy was called for the examination of discovery, she explained that she was extremely uncomfortable with being placed in such a momentous position. It was decided by Locas and his advisors that Nancy would not have to name any players. Locas absorbed a few days' criticism in the press when he disclosed this decision. Members of the media, who were also anticipating hardhitting and controversial recommendations, were in for a further letdown.

At the end of September, Locas made a single recommendation: "That the directors of the [ambulance company], and police of L'Ancienne Lorette take the necessary measures to help [their respective] ambulance technicians get a proper, special education on the effects of toxication by cocaine, and what proper acts should be done, and what proper manoeuvres should be taken to minimize the danger—all this for a better protection of human life."

Following a chronology of John's last 24 hours, and an overview of his life leading up to the event of his death, which he subtitled "A Sad Year," Locas closed his text with his conclusions on all aspects of John's death.

The coroner said that while he could not conclude steroids caused John's death directly, "the nature of using steroids can bring on situations that will favorize certain other causes to direct death."

Locas based his findings on expert testimony and excerpts from several authoritative studies on steroids. He wrote that steroids "brought John to start taking cocaine, and it was cocaine that caused his death," then requalified that statement by saying he could only hypothesize.

Forensic toxicologists testified that John had a cocaine concentration of 0.13 mg per 100 ml of blood in his system—a level that is lethal. Based on this evidence, and testimony that John used cocaine regularly, Locas portrayed the last moments of John's life: His agitated state, brought on by the level of cocaine in his system, "gave the subject an acute need for oxygen. In the case of Kordic, when he was put on the floor in hotel room 205, not only was he not able to get the oxygen he needed, but pressure put on his back by the policeman . . . didn't help him to breathe properly, and in fact, it stopped him from breathing properly.

"The same result occurred when they [police] tied his hands behind his back. This put pressure on his chest . . . his heart became more contracted and the blood did not circulate well—flowing in another direction toward his lungs to promote the pulmonary edema which brought the asphyxia that caused his death."

Locas, however, concluded that the police intervention was justified and that it followed guidelines in police training to the letter.

The inquiry heard from expert witness Pierre Remiard, who had been a special consultant to the Quebec police institute for 11 years, and was considered an expert in the teaching of police education and police matters. He was also a former member of the Montreal police force, the French national police, and had served on an international expert committee, under former U.N. Secretary General Javier Perez De Cuellar, that helped create a civilian police force in San Salvador in 1991.

Remiard was called upon to outline the regimen of an officer's training. He explained that an officer falls into one of five zones of mental preparation on his job. The zones are coded by colors—a white zone for off-duty, yellow for calmness, orange for awareness of situation, red at the scene of a crime, and finally black for extreme situations prompting the use of force or a weapon. Correspondingly, there are six degrees of suspect behavior which the officer must gauge in affecting an arrest, Remiard explained. They also range from mild to extreme exhibitions.

Locas drew on Remiard's testimony to conclude that the police were unapologetically correct in their actions the night John died. They observed standards of conduct in dealing with an intoxicated person. They ordered John to leave the room, did not listen to his insults, and did not ridicule the suspect. They then moved quickly to "protect people around the suspect and the suspect, too." They practiced the correct technique in arresting a suspect of John's strength, getting him onto the floor, facedown, so he could not see who was controlling him, Locas said. The focus was to direct the suspect's strength downward, toward the floor, then cuff the hands, and avoid hitting or punching. John's strength was also justification for the immobilization technique of placing a knee on one of the centers of rotation, the neck or the hips. "Here again, the way the policemen worked conformed to the way they were taught," Locas wrote.

Sergeant Poulain also complied with police training in taking the suspect to hospital "once [suspect] is bound and loses contact with reality or shows signs of problems."

Locas introduced a special section in the report to deal with the testimony of Desrosiers, "who apparently saw Sergeant Janvier standing on John Kordic's body for about ten seconds with a smile on his face like the smile of a hunter at a safari, proud of what he just got."

He referred to the section as dealing with the "Safari Pose," and wrote: "The event, if we should accept it for real, would not conform to the teachings given at the police institute in Quebec. It would also be very detrimental as far as the level of medical causes of death to the victim, but experts Remiard and Blais [toxicologist René Blais] did not comment on what the witness said . . . and neither did lawyers present. But newspapers talked about it at length and this is why I must explain why this testimony cannot be kept.

"First of all, it is inconceivable that such an enormous and indecent gesture could have been done by a superior officer in the presence of nine other policemen . . . and of the nine, four were from another police corps . . . and two ambulance technicians.

"Second, Officer Janvier had no reason to do this 'Safari Pose' because he had never been provoked or pushed around or insulted by the victim.

"Thirdly, no other witnesses present saw this gesture . . . none of the other nine officers . . . other ambulance personnel or Martin Bouchard, or others standing in the hallway.

"Also, it's inconceivable that the witness never spoke of this extraordinary event to any of his colleagues . . . and also to police investigating from the QPP who interrogated him . . . nor anyone else until he testified eight months later."

Locas summarized by stating that a "balance" between the officer's judgment of the suspect and the consequences of his actions was maintained in the arrest.

"What the policeman did to restrain John on the floor using pressure on his body was proportionate to the resistance that John was giving and also of the dangerous aspect of the suspect. They didn't hit him in any way . . . no firearms were used . . . Unfortunately, seeing as they ignored all the medical process bringing on a pulmonary edema [cocaine, plus agitation, plus lack of oxygen], they couldn't guess their actions . . . could bring on the medical risk of loss of life.

"And even if they had known it, it's not said that the degree of danger in the suspect couldn't justify it. So there is no need to intervene, to modify the teachings [of the police] or how they function or the methods of police intervention that were used in the John Kordic case."

The first and only segment of the report in which the coroner cast a slight shadow of doubt on the techniques used in arresting John was when he addressed the intervention of the ambulance technicians.

He drew on testimony from toxicologist René Blais, who was a member of his advisory staff, which also included Quebec lawyer Jean-Guy Picard and QPP investigating officer Michel Pageau.

Blais told the inquiry that John's life depended on how quick the police and ambulance technicians were to recognize his need for oxygen. The toxicologist stated flatly that John should have been given oxygen much sooner than he was. John should also have been further examined in the room, turned onto his back, and his hands uncuffed to facilitate easier breathing, he said.

The process of reanimation would then have begun sooner, Blais added.

Locas referred to Blais's testimony indirectly in considering the lack of proper assessment of John's condition when the hockey player lay bound on the carpet at the Maxim. He observed that Desrosiers could not exact an assessment because of the turmoil of the police activity in subduing John. That point raised a curious contrast to Desrosiers's testimony, and to what Locas himself described in detailing John's last moments. Locas wrote that Desrosiers felt "shoved" around when he entered the room. At that time, the police were fully involved with John, and had him facedown, cuffed, and roped off at the ankles. In his description of the scene, though, Locas notes that John was immobilized by the bindings, had a 200-pound-plus officer kneeling on his neck, another holding his head down, and another holding down his legs. John was also, in Locas's descriptions, a ghastly blue color, almost unconscious, with a mixture of a white bubbly liquid and blood dribbling from his mouth. In reference to the same moment, Desrosiers said he was shoved by police, and not by any action from, or reaction to, John. Desrosiers also testified that it was at that time he noticed Janvier in the Safari Pose on top of John's back.

Locas noted the career experiences of the three men in the room with ambulance-technician training—Desrosiers, his partner Benoit Nadeau, and Sergeant Poulain. In doing so, he referred to the minimal teachings each received on the subject of the effects of cocaine on a suspect/patient. He then wrote: "If I look back on what's been said [in the inquiry], the fact that the ambulance technicians didn't give oxygen to John sooner . . . wouldn't prompt any questions on their competence. It was the absence of their knowledge in this situation . . . their ignorance in this case is due to a lack of information they received during training."

In his general summaries, Locas wrote: "The state of Kordic was probably compromised in an irreversible way and nothing permits us to conclude a change of seating position [from facedown to sitting upright] could have changed something in what happened."

Locas concurred with a doctor who testified that the positioning of John on the stretcher, facedown and head-first down the stairway, was irrelevant to the inquiry's purposes. Blais, however, testified that the procedure contributed to an abnormal flow of a foreign substance, namely food, into the lungs so that the substance would then be wrongly introduced into the respiratory tract.

By the time John arrived at the hospital, he had been under full cardiac arrest for at least 10 minutes, Locas noted. "If we want to avoid irreversible damage, basic [CPR] manoeuvres must be administered in the first four minutes of a cardiac arrest, and advanced manoeuvres in the first eight minutes. This means that [John's] chances of having a normal life, if ever he had survived, were nil."

When he finally released his report, Locas dutifully stood before a press corps bent on criticizing its apparent shortcomings. Locas had completed the second longest public inquiry in Quebec history. It was arguably among the province's most controversial. In his mind, it was complete and irreproachable.

Locas was frequently called upon by Quebec chief coroner Jean Grenier to preside over inquiries in the Quebec City area. He had presided over two previous inquests, both regarding citizens who were struck and killed by police cruisers. It was his mandate under the Quebec coroner's act to determine the cause of death, define the circumstances surrounding it, and make recommendations where he judged there to be a necessity. He assumed the role of a judge in having the final word on the incident of John's death, although he could not by definition find blame in any of the parties involved.

On August 11, 1992, Grenier announced that his investigating coroner, Dr. Pierre Charles Samson, "could see no utility in holding an inquiry." Samson arrived at his decision "because he had good cooperation with the witnesses," Grenier said. Samson would await toxicological results and an internal report from the QPP before making a final decision.

The same day, Andres Arturs, the popular talk-show host and broadcaster for CHRC in Quebec, lashed out at Grenier with one of his patented on-air tirades. He has a flatly sarcastic manner of speaking, a no-nonsense approach to calling the kettle black if he saw it as such, which made him widely popular with Quebeckers. Arturs condemned Grenier's decision as the chief coroner's way to rule out in advance the truth of the police intervention. His most stirring comment was a suggestion that the number of police in John's room alone was enough to prompt the public to suspect, simply, that "the cops killed him."

On September 12, Grenier cited popular sentiments held by radio personalities and the print media as a factor in his desire to produce an undisputed record of the facts in John Kordic's death.

"It's clear now that . . . the verdict is coming out in the public," Grenier told reporters. "There's a risk of confusion and injustice. People have rights to their opinion, but it doesn't make any sense to leave any doubts in this death."

Virtually every major news outlet in Quebec converged on the inquiry, as well as several newspapers from across Canada. There were hundreds more stories written on John, based on the testimony. The Quebec media carried live reports and comprehensive daily coverage, while Canadian Press dispatched daily stories across the country on its wire service.

Arturs, however, and to a lesser extent Jean Perron at CJRP were the barometers of criticism and the sources of statements that the print media couldn't publish. Arturs dispatched his own A-list reporter, Martin Paquette, to cover the proceedings. Paquette was a former police officer who dabbled in free-lance reporting until a permanent, and better-paying, position was offered to him.

Arturs had long been a thorn in the side of politicians, police, coroners, and virtually any public figure in the news of the day. He was regarded as the Howard Stern of

Quebec radio. He sharpened his wit daily on his victims, and was threatened with lawsuits so many times he forgot most of them.

Arturs embellished most the testimony during the Kordic inquest with his own reflections. He pondered on-air what the police were thinking. What prompted such quick and drastic intervention? he asked. John wasn't holding any hostages . . . and what happened to the element of negotiation? Why not leave him alone until he settled down? Everyone present knew who he was, and John certainly wasn't in any condition to make an escape.

While much of the testimony was tedious and technical, lawyers from the police and ambulance services ultimately butted heads in reproaching one another's clients. Shouting matches erupted during questioning, reflecting an attempt on one side to shed the notion of blame to the other. Police lawyers emphatically insisted that John was alive on the stretcher, and when he was placed into the ambulance. They raised doubts over the timing in the first delivery of oxygen to John. In counterattacks, ambulance lawyers said complaints about John came from the front desk, not patrons of the hotel. They postulated that the police plan all along was to effect a strong-armed takedown on John and bring him to hospital, not police headquarters. There was a tremendous level of anxiety over the public's perception of which side was beyond reproach, despite the fact that Locas could not point a finger of blame at anyone.

Bouchard, the Kordic family lawyer, waded into the middle of the bickering. He provided the most telling moments in the inquest during cross-examination of Sergeant Poulain.

"Sergeant, when you were called to the hotel, you knew who the person was in room 205 . . . ?"

"Yes, we knew it was John Kordic."

"Was he posing a danger to himself?"

"No, not exactly."

"Was he threatening any other patrons of the hotel?"

"No."

"Did you order the arrest because he threatened the police?"

"No, we did not."

"Why did you order the arrest at that moment?"

"I'm not exactly sure . . ."

Bouchard focused his questioning on what appeared to be loopholes in the arresting officers' accounts of their conduct. Bouchard exposed the first indication of a police cover-up when he asked for a police copy of transcripts of radio talk between police the night John died. Bouchard, who most observers credited with the most competent performance among the lawyers at the inquest, had enlisted the services of an audio specialist with expertise in examining such tapes. The expert discovered what he believed to be a breach in the tapes, and concluded that a portion of the record had been either erased or cut out and the tape spliced together again.

Locas called for a sidebar between Bouchard and the police lawyers. He then reserved his decision on the admissibility of the police transcripts until after a lunch-hour recess. When the inquest resumed, he denied Bouchard's request.

The press immediately attacked the decision, and suspected complicity between Locas and the police lawyers. Paquette, who was seated near the lawyers' desks, witnessed what he thought was an open act of indiscretion between the two parties. He went on the air later that day and described how he saw Picard subtly wink at the police lawyer, as if to acknowledge that some clandestine favor had been consummated in having the transcripts rejected as evidence. "I couldn't believe what I was seeing," he said on-air.

When asked for comments on the alleged wink, Bouchard chose to respect the honor of the bar above entangling himself and the cause of the Kordic family in a controversy over something he never witnessed.

Paquette, however, developed very strong convictions about the mind-set of the police during John's arrest. Drawing on his own nine-year experience as an officer, he decided that the police intention was to teach John a lesson since the hockey player had been the subject of previous complaints.

When Locas released his report, the press took his lone recommendation as the final indignity in a toothless inquest. Locas was far more emphatic about the amount of cocaine in John's body than about any of the other extenuating circumstances on the night of August 8, 1992. While it was part of the press's mandate to criticize him, there could be no mistaking that Locas had been converted to believe the police and ambulance technicians could not be faulted. He admitted to friends in private that he'd shared the public's predisposition about the number of police in John's room. After he released his report, though, he acknowledged that the expert testimony on behalf of the police had convinced him that John was solely responsible for his own demise. It was as if he had taken the place of the judge and jury. It also lent an air of the macabre to his intentions of defining the tragedy in as humane terms as possible: since John was not capable of killing himself, the world which he surrounded himself with had edged him out; the police, the ambulance technicians, and John himself, were all merely playing out their roles.

In February 1993, long before the inquest was over, the Kordic family announced that they were filing a $1.6 million lawsuit against the police, ambulance, and City of Quebec. Bouchard was roundly criticized by police lawyers for using the inquiry as a testing ground for his theories and evidence. Bouchard, though, measured those sentiments against the burden of the Kordic family. Regina was present throughout the inquest, and was joined by her daughters Toni and Lillian. She sat with headphones on, listening to English translations of the testimony, and sometimes raged aloud at comments from the arresting officers. In other moments, she sobbed when the understanding of a terrible moment gripped her. Most observers wondered where she drew her strength from. She had precious little time to mourn the loss of her son.

Some reporters even thought her eyes were dry when she cried.

Epilogue

ON FEBRUARY 27, 1995, Paul Bouchard received a communiqué from lawyers representing the two police forces involved in John's August 8, 1992, arrest. It contained the beginning of the end of the Kordic family's lawsuit—a directive outlining the desire of senior police officials to settle the lawsuit out of court.

There had been no leak to the press regarding the police overture: veteran cop-beat reporters were unaware of the development. A tip like this, however, would likely not have rekindled the kind of interest that had surrounded the affair at its zenith. John had long since passed on, and so had the hype and controversy surrounding his death. All that remained was his family's desire to see an end to the lawsuit.

Bouchard initially welcomed the opportunity to proceed in a media vacuum. He would not, and could not, publicly discuss any details of the proceedings. Bouchard, who couldn't reveal evidence that had not yet been introduced in court, had enlisted the services of an expert from New York who helped him expose loopholes in the police testimony and evidence given during the Kordic inquest. From the moment the offer of an out-of-court settlement was received, it was obvious that the new evidence was significant enough to prompt the police response. Bouchard remained in contact with his police counterparts for the better part of two months after the original offer. He could only say a settlement was at hand, and if not, a writ would be dropped and the lawsuit would proceed to court—likely in the fall. Beyond that, his only comment was that he would have definite statements to make regarding a police cover-up.

For all his painstaking effort to expose the police evidence in the Kordic inquest, Bouchard weighed the relative benefits of the police offer. As much as he was committed to the case, he couldn't help feeling that accepting a settlement would be in the family's best interests. For the better part of 30 months, the family's grief had been perpetuated by the legal proceedings necessary to get at the truth of how John died. Every time Regina had to come to Toronto, her suffering was evident. During one visit, while she was walking through Pearson International Airport, she happened to cross paths with Don Cherry. Without saying a word, and seeing what she was enduring, Cherry—a good friend of the family's—put his arm around her, pulling her close as they walked through the airport. Like Cherry, Bouchard was conscious of Regina's prolonged suffering; it seemed that an out-of-court settlement would bring about the most pain-free conclusion; it would also help the family get on with their lives.

The breadth of Bouchard's case covered the police conduct at the Maxim Motel. He was proceeding on the premise that the police testimony and evidence at the Kordic inquest represented only *half* of what had actually happened the night John died.

There was enough to suggest a veiled truth about the police response in the personal hell Desrosiers endured throughout the inquest.

A deeply devoted family man, Desrosiers woke up one day shortly after his "Safari Pose" testimony and left home. Reacting to extreme stress, he left behind a pregnant wife and a son, who endured negative attention at school as his father's behavior made headlines. After his testimony, Desrosiers began encountering indignant looks, even threatening behavior from the local police. When he responded to calls, police at the scene would often stare rudely at him, mutter snide comments, or refuse to work with him. He eventually filed for workers' compensation to cover the time he spent away from his job and family.

Even that was almost denied him when the ambulance company and the province argued over who was going to make the payments.

Desrosiers eventually returned to his family, and to his job. To this day, however, he still meets with the odd icy stare from police. Only the people he made contact with every day knew about his personal ordeal. Had more people known, and his story been pursued further, he might have been fingered as one of the few non-police witnesses who suppressed the truth of John's death. When asked in a January 1995 interview about the possibility that he had not told everything he saw, he answered curtly, "No. There is nothing more." Yet, he also acknowledged that, in a similar situation in the future, he would react differently. "[The police] are gonna be surprised," he said. More than anything, though, Desrosiers wished to forget the name John Kordic.

In December 1994, renewed interest in the Kordic case surfaced with the press coverage of the sensational trial of five Montreal police officers on charges of assault causing bodily harm. Files from the Kordic inquest were pulled for possible reference in arguments of law during the trial, which centered on Richard Barnabé, a 38-year-old taxi driver who fell into a coma during 80 minutes in police custody on December 14, 1993.

On that date, Barnabé, during an alleged robbery attempt, broke a church window and led police on a ten-kilometer chase before he was arrested. According to media reports, he was bleeding when brought to Police Station 44. An ambulance attendant said he saw police officers enter Barnabé's prison cell. The attendant also said that, shortly afterward, he was on the phone with a doctor, and heard Barnabé scream so loudly the doctor could hear it through the phone. At 5:00 a.m., a police officer asked someone to take Barnabé's pulse. By that time, Barnabé was unconscious, and his pulse weak. He was taken to hospital at 5:06 a.m. where he was diagnosed as comatose.

The Barnabé family filed a $7.95-million civil suit against ten police officers, five of whom would ultimately face the assault charges.

The passions around the case intensified in the city—indeed, across the nation—when the media began to run pictures of Barnabé's battered and swollen face, as he lay in a coma. Video footage of his mouth, gaping slightly, and his transfixed gaze—while lying in a hospital bed—was also broadcast to viewers. It was a disturbing image: one that became indelibly linked to the city's police force.

The police damage-control response was left, in part, to Yves Prud'Homme, the tough-talking head of the police union, who lashed back at what he felt was sensationalistic media coverage of the Barnabé case.

"It's true a picture is worth a thousand words," he told reporters at the time. "If all citizens listened to an order from a police officer, life would be beautiful. But that's not exactly the case." Prud'Homme postulated that, with about two million calls a year, the situation may arise when a police officer "commits an error in good faith . . . take a walk in the emergency rooms and see how many errors are made there. You have to make a distinction between malice and an error done in good faith."

It was inevitable that the Barnabé case would recall other controversies circulating about a city police force that had been the subject of five independent inquiries in the previous eight years. The most recent probe—in July 1993—had been commissioned by the Quebec government. The findings stressed that the union representing the city's 4,450 officers had grown too powerful, which prompted speculation about the chief's authority over the force. All members of the police force remained defiant. On February 13, 1992, they had marched in the streets of Montreal to protest critical remarks made by Chief Alain St. Germain. It marked the first time in Canadian history that police officers demanded the resignation of their own chief of police. St. Germain released a scathing report against tactical-squad officers for the shooting death of Marcellus Francois, a black man who was mistaken for a drug dealer. (It was the Francois case that sparked the Canada Day riots near Labonte's apartment, when John sprang from the balcony to rescue François Labonte from an angry mob of youths.)

In Quebec City, public scrutiny of the local and provincial police force reached a definitive focus in *Quebecgate*, an exposé of corruption in politics and police forces in Quebec, written in 1989 by former St. Foy detective John Tardiff. The book created a scandal, and gave radio talk-show hosts like Arturs plenty of ammunition to satirize a host of high-profile Quebeckers. Among the many subjects in his book, Tardiff targeted Jean Grenier for having, in his opinion, a criminal responsibility in the death of his wife. Grenier was cleared of any wrongdoing, and no inquest was ever called, after Madeleine Grenier died from a bullet wound while on a 1966 hunting trip. Grenier's public reputation, though, was tainted, especially in light of remarks from Arturs, who, after referring to the incident, questioned the public's trust in the provincial coroner's office.

Tardiff raised the case on several occasions with senior officers from his own force. In 1989, he recounted every piece of evidence he had accumulated on a five-hour-long tape. He then presented his findings to St. Foy police chief Ronald Bourget, who had preceded St. Germain as chief of police in Montreal. Tardiff, however, said he was told to pull the plug on his proceedings, or face disciplinary action. He ultimately left the force in 1989, at loggerheads with Bourget over the case.

When his book hit the stands, Tardiff was served with a notice from Grenier's lawyer, Guy Bertrand, outlining a possible lawsuit. In the notice, Tardiff was ordered to have the book removed from the shelves or face litigation. Tardiff responded by calling a press conference inviting Grenier and Bertrand to debate his findings. Tardiff characterized the affair as an advent for an "interrogatoire au préable," or prior interrogation, an interview session arranged by police for all suspects and witnesses in a crime trial. "Bertrand backed out," he said in a January 1995 interview. "I had the questions the QPP wanted to ask him all along."

Grenier relinquished his post before the Kordic inquest reached its conclusion, and became a highly influential player in the province's bid for the 2002 Olympics. His move was timely as much as it was opportunistic. His name was never mentioned in any of the criticism directed at the other key players in the inquest. It is almost assured that he can never be harmed again by what is recorded on Tardiff's tape. (Tardiff has since, in some respects, graduated to a successful partnership in a performance/athletic drink company, and is despised by enough former colleagues to ensure he will never return to the ranks of the police again.)

Only Paul Bouchard, on one side, and ten arresting officers on the other can reveal what really happened to John the night he died. Bouchard has sufficiently unnerved the police, prompting their bid to settle out of court. Beyond that, he can only deal with their offer, and with the Kordic family's concerns, all in the context of the healing powers of time. The police, for their part, have not escaped unscathed. There had been a relatively small leak regarding the arrest and takedown at the Maxim Motel. Actually, it was more the case of a few words passed between officers, over drinks, long after John was laid in the earth.

According to sources who heard the stories, there are at least two officers who are living with "hard feelings" over John's death. These officers revealed to confidants, "We did wrong by that boy," and "There's no reason for him to die."

According to the same sources, John was only told why he was under arrest after he was lying on the carpet, unconscious, and well into the first throes of death—a detail that contrasts dramatically with the version given during the inquest.

There is also the suggestion that considerably more harm was inflicted on John's body than Desrosiers's "Safari Pose" testimony indicated. Again, according to sources, John was virtually dying when voices shouted at him "Mon Christe d'écourant," and "Mon tabarnacle de gros cochon." The first phrase, loosely translated, means, "You—the person you are inside—are disgusting; a loser," (although the French meaning carries significantly more weight and conviction than the English translation ever could). The second phrase translates as: "You big fucking pig." Also, according to the sources, there was a consensus in the room that "We are going to show you how we function."

Bouchard, although bound by duty to protect his evidence, was able to corroborate these stories, in part, when they were presented to him. He even went so far as to say, "Some of that is 100 percent accurate." He also supported another piece of information from the sources that the testimony given by police at the inquest represented only 50 percent of what actually happened that night at the Maxim Motel.

There are many people who continue to say prayers for John; there are also many who believe John should still be here today. If the truth of how John died is carried in that belief, then who is to say the sins that were committed that night are not any less terrible now, that his story is over.

John is buried next to his father at the top of a small hill in St. Albert's Cemetery. After his funeral, an unidentified woman was seen by his grave. Bryan Fogarty, who can no longer talk about the life he shared with John, was also reported to have visited the grave site, just before his own life turned around, for the better.

One day, all those who loved him will find out if John rests in peace, but the ground around him will remain unquiet until the questions about how he died are answered.

Appendix

THE NATIONAL HOCKEY League was spared the embarrassment of a public inquiry into drug use among its players. Such a probe was earnestly considered—and very nearly acted upon—as an appendage to the John Kordic inquest. Only a last-minute change of heart by Coroner Locas preempted the sending of subpoenas to players and management with the Quebec Nordiques, the Montreal Canadiens, and the NHL head offices.

Locas and his team of advisors—Picard, Blais, and QPP officer Pageau—had prepared a detailed dossier in advance of a possible NHL drug probe. It fell on Picard to consider all legal avenues from which they, as a team, could proceed.

The dossier was built on investigative work done by Pageau. Prior to the opening of the inquest, Pageau gathered information based on interviews with Nancy Masse, experts on steroid and cocaine use, and with NHL lawyers. He gained as firm an understanding as he possibly could of the way the NHL handled players with drug problems. He found member teams assuming virtually 100 percent of the responsibility of actually learning about a problem, as well as for the follow-up rehabilitation.

As word of the impending probe spread, Picard was contacted by more than a dozen experts in the fields of sport psychology and steroid use who offered themselves as expert witnesses. Picard knew he had the full cooperation of the Canadian Centre for Drug-Free Sport, which had had a huge stake in the Dubin Inquiry into the Ben Johnson scandal. He also made contact with "people in Ottawa," although he would not confirm whether they were lawyers or politicians.

When Pageau delivered his findings, Picard was left to deliberate two binding facts that would drive the eventual decision on whether or not to proceed with the probe: his paramount piece of evidence would be Nancy's testimony—and was that enough to proceed with "getting into the players' locker room and the NHL president's office" under Quebec law.

Picard had the advantage of working within the parameters of civil law—as opposed to criminal law. The Kordic inquest fell under the realm of civil law, which is distinct in the way evidence engenders proof. In criminal law, the degree of proof required is absolute—de facto—while in civil law, proof is argued in terms of certainties and probabilities versus possibilities. It was within the context of certainties, probabilities and possibilities that Picard had to find enough evidence to couple to Nancy's testimony, and prompt the Kordic inquest to begin subpoenaing NHL witnesses.

Picard returned to his own law practice on Bouvier Road in Quebec City to initiate research into the effects of steroids on hard-core users. He was going to proceed on the theory that people who abuse one illegal substance generally compound it by abusing a second illegal substance at the same time. He drew on experts and expert opinion from medical and doctoral dissertations which proved steroid use was widespread in sports. "The proof was made of the usage of steroids as being widespread in sports," he said in an interview. "If we could prove taking steroids encouraged the consumption of cocaine . . . seeing as how cocaine caused (John's) death . . . we would have had the legal right to go into the NHL."

Picard, though, ran into myriad legal hurdles that would ultimately influence the decision to probe the NHL. Picard was armed with two certainties: that steroids affected John's health, but were not probable in the cause of death; and the use of cocaine "killed John, according to experts, and according to all probability," but its widespread use in the NHL was not probable according to the same experts.

"So, in the question of steroids in sports, while it may be prevalent, if it does not immediately cause death, it is out of the coroner's hands," Picard said. "If we could have proved steroids caused John's death . . . we would have been able to go farther."

In considering the probe from the angle of cocaine use among NHL players, Picard encountered a similar barrier. "We had proof he [John] used coke, and that it caused his death . . . but we couldn't establish it was widespread in the NHL," he continued. "We needed this proof before we could probe the NHL's players and people. We couldn't just assume so and begin calling witnesses.

"We knew steroids were being used in professional sports, but they did not cause the death we were considering. On a parallel, cocaine was used (by John) and it was the cause of death, but the proof was that it was possible, but not probable in the NHL. Therefore, it was possible that cocaine was used in the NHL but we did not have the judicial power to explore it."

Experts suggested that several factors in the lifestyles of NHL players made them easy targets for cocaine dealers. The experts told Picard that the players are "high risk" people because of the money, level of stress, young age, and constant movement and exposure to big cities. Picard, though, faced a further dilemma in not having the legal means to gain access to drug-testing information, the way he would have at the amateur sport level. In the Ben Johnson scandal, Johnson's test history was administered by the federal government, and could be made public in an inquiry. No such provision existed for professional team sports in Canada or the United States.

Picard was made to understand by the experts that each NHL team had its own strategies to respond to player drug problems. He was convinced of the effectiveness of the strategies, but could not legally prompt any team to turn over documentation. After considering all the information and evidence, Picard reluctantly gave up on his initiative to subpoena NHL witnesses. He also acknowledged that his statements to the press regarding the NHL probe were premature.

"Despite the NHL Players' Association stance against this type of control [drug testing], I am convinced that they [NHL teams] do it," he said. "After all this time, and even though we could not legally go into the NHL, I have a halfway satisfaction that it (drug testing) was being done in a censored way, by the teams.

"I am no dumbie in this case, either. I admit there is a deception here based on the fact that we were not able to legally go into the system . . . but my deception would have been larger if I didn't believe the team did this work to control the abuse of drugs."

Picard was ultimately left with the uncomfortable feeling of being gun-shy. What he did have was Nancy's knowledge about other players taking cocaine with John. Whether she named names or not, Picard was within proper legal proximity of launching an NHL probe. He would not have directed Pageau to investigate the NHL, nor his own office staff to contact experts across Canada and the United States, if he did not feel justified. Over the course of this initiative, though, he became the reluctant captain of an undermanned, underpowered ship in a rough sea.

"We asked the experts to prove that taking steroids had a link to taking cocaine," he said. "We had some proof, but it was insufficient. For example, taking steroids is illegal. Socially and psychologically, it has been proved that if you take something illegal, you will take other things that are illegal as well. If they [players] live in a marginal society where they come in contact with people who sell steroids, it increases the risk they'll be exposed to people who sell cocaine. There was never enough legal proof that a user of steroids could necessarily become a user of cocaine. When you use steroids, it's not like using cocaine, you do not become dependent on steroids. You can do so on cocaine. From there, the impossibility evolved of getting into the NHL, because steroid use could not be linked to use of cocaine, and there, the impossibility of proving cocaine was widespread in the NHL.

"We were tied up by legal considerations. People were

saying finally someone was going to probe pro sports and clean it up. But we were legally constrained by the proof given. We could not go on what Nancy said as being a possibility.

"Because of the pressure of the media and the general population, we created what the people expected. I remember creating hopes in the press . . . that there was this possibility."

Picard also said that the QPP "did not want to go to war with the NHL . . . Pageau wanted to be as objective as possible, in case we would have to deal with Ottawa [the federal government] . . . We prepared the turf so we could go into the NHL if a higher authority [felt there was enough evidence to do so]."

Picard's burden was somewhat lessened by a concurrent criminal investigation that threatened to absorb the entire Kordic inquiry. On October 17, 1992, Operation Chacal, the drug sweep conducted by the Gendarme Royale du Canada (RCMP), netted 40 arrests in a series of raids and warrants that also forced the closure of l'Acropole. Among those arrested were two women, one of them 19 years old, who admitted selling cocaine to John Kordic, up to six days before his death. As stories of the arrests appeared in the papers, concern grew over a possible overlapping of legal jurisdictions between Operation Chacal and the Kordic inquest. Locas said in an interview in September 1994 that the advisory team feared arguments could be brought forward to link the NHL probe to the realm of criminal law. Had the argument been successful, Locas said, there was an additional fear that the Kordic inquest would have been assimilated by Operation Chacal.

At that time, rumors surfaced in the Quebec media that Grenier had put pressure on Locas to wrap up the Kordic inquest as quickly as possible to avoid such a development. By the time Locas was writing his report, Grenier had relinquished his post, and had gone on to head the province's bid for the 2002 Winter Olympics.

For all its hype, the John Kordic inquiry was put to bed with a relative whimper. The coroner's single recommendation alone prompted sufficient derision in the press. Then there was the hollow ring of the suggestion that the

NHL could be probed for drug use. Among the final observations was the introspection of some media regulars at the inquest that perhaps the high expectations were solely the creation of the press.

Underneath it all, there was John, long gone, and quickly fading from the hearts and minds of everyone but his family and close friends. So many of them remembered what they were doing when a voice on the radio or television informed the world of his death. Along with the shock and tears, there were personal reflections of John. The preciousness of memory was all anyone had left.

After John's death, and on its two anniversaries, the press appropriately discussed the impact it was having on promoting a comprehensive drug policy in the NHL. Most writers urged the NHL to finally come to its senses and develop such a policy. The mood for change had indeed arrived with the new NHL commissioner Gary Bettman, who hinted at a new era in the way he handled Bob Probert's dangerous relapse into alcohol and cocaine abuse during the summer of 1994.

Actually, the NHL players' union had been consulting the players about developing a new drug policy as far back as 1990, after Bob Goodenow replaced Alan Eagleson as executive director of the NHLPA.

Goodenow was highly regarded for his experience as a labor lawyer and player agent. Based in Detroit, he'd represented 20 NHL players, including Brett Hull. Prior to managing professional athletes, he was a labor lawyer, and had captained the Harvard hockey team in the mid-1970s. He was among the six candidates to replace Eagleson, who met with a mini-revolt in the fall of 1988. Eagleson's leadership was challenged by player agents Ron Salcer, Rich Winter, and former NFL union boss Ed Garvey, and he agreed to step aside during a complete review of his tenure. Eagleson weathered the storm, in large part thanks to a meeting in August 1989 during which no financial wrongdoing was uncovered. Eagleson, though, who had maintained his player-agent business throughout his tenure, agreed to relinquish control of it and gradually surrender the reins of the union.

Goodenow immediately took conciliatory measures on

behalf of the players, with regards to their discussions on drug-related issues at membership meetings.

In 1992, he represented the players at the now-infamous Collective Bargaining Agreement (CBA) talks, which resulted in the owners locking out the players during the Stanley Cup play-offs. The press dutifully lamented the madness in the prospect of losing the postseason. At the outset of the negotiations, though, Goodenow tabled before the NHL owners a historic first proposal for a new drug policy:

"We made a proposal regarding a drug and alcohol program," Goodenow said in a 1995 interview. "It was progressive in nature . . . It had everything, treatment, aftercare, 1-800 numbers, people assigned to take calls . . . It was progressive, multi-strike.

"This was before John Kordic's death. It was a subject the players were talking a lot about. We had retained experts to advise us, had surveys sent out to the membership. It became an issue for bargaining.

"We were told by John Ziegler and the owners it was too expensive . . . were told by the owners' side in the bargaining that what we wanted implemented was too expensive."

The advent of a new drug-policy proposal, and its refusal, were never reported on at the time. If implemented, the proposal itself ranged in the neighborhood of $250,000. It was more appropriate that it remain the best-kept secret of those negotiations, based on its ignominious reception. The union, though, maintained efforts to explore the drug issues concerning its players.

While cost concerns figured into virtually all CBA negotiations, the NHL's response was more reflective of an attitude harbored as far back as the late 1950s when Ziegler was climbing the management ladder.

A young lawyer from a firm representing the Detroit Red Wings, Ziegler became a fixture in that organization by the mid-1960s. He bought a condo in North Miami, Florida, next door to team owner Bruce Norris, which positioned him more favorably than the rest of Norris's cronies. By 1966, he had gained an appointment to the team's board of directors, and became the Wings' alternate

NHL governor. In 1977, he emerged as one of three candidates to replace Clarence Campbell for the NHL presidency. None of the candidates—Ziegler, James Cullen, and Bob Sedgewick, all lawyers for NHL teams—commanded backing from a majority of NHL owners. Ziegler, though, had Norris and Chicago Blackhawks owner Bill Wirtz—considered the two most powerful men in hockey—in his corner, and in September, he won the top post in hockey.

Ziegler took aim at several clear targets—scaling back player gains in the CBA as much as possible, acquiring a U.S. television contract, and coaxing the Canadian teams to share in the wealth of their broadcast deal. Throughout his legal training, though, and his subsequent rise to power in the NHL, he retained a very distinct governing philosophy—and applied it to his handling of players with drug problems.

"Most of my practice was in courtrooms, Anglo-American jurisprudence," Ziegler said in a January 1995 interview. "Our legal systems in Canada and the U.S. are descendants of the common law system from England.

"I represented Detroit in 1959. I began to have a feeling of how owners were feeling with respect to an issue like this [drugs]. In the mid-1960s, you have concern over abuse of illegal prescription drugs. For years in the NHL, there had been specific requirements with respect to prescription drugs . . . notices put in dressing rooms, a very elaborate monitoring system.

"In the '60s, the San Diego Chargers football-team doctor went to jail in a scandal over players using prescription drugs. Out of that came a bylaw with very specific guidelines for prescription drugs. There had to be an inventory of what was legal and illegal. It was no longer acceptable for that to be in the hands of team trainers. The handling [of prescription drugs] was done by team doctors.

"The next step, logistically, was simply that you shouldn't be using drugs at all . . . It wasn't something I created. It was my judgment of what the philosophy of the NHL was. We were not an entertainment that was going to tolerate young athletes using drugs and play a game where the result would be in doubt, and people paying money to see that result.

"Every time you do an illegal drug, a dust speck of cocaine, you are breaking the law and I wanted to uphold the law.

"When a case came before me, it wasn't a case of first impression. I had been on the board of governors for 11 years, since 1966. I felt, though, in terms of the integrity of the game, of what we stood for, you couldn't be a little bit pregnant. It was a black-and-white issue. If you were going to use illegal drugs, you should find work somewhere else."

Ziegler never felt it necessary to develop a drug policy to insert into the text of the CBA. Instead, when the first case of player drug use came before the league, Ziegler invoked Bylaw 17(3) and framed a ruling around his judgment.

In 1979, the NHL took its first initiatives towards providing resources for players with drug problems. League vice president Brian O'Neil, together with NHL security officials, compiled a list of treatment centers and programs throughout the United States. The information was packaged and sent to the member clubs as an "informational device" for response to player drug problems.

"There were treatment centers in New England and Hazelden," Ziegler said. "We collected information on these treatment centers and outreach programs, and put it in the hands of our clubs, so they'd have access to them and the services they provide. The NHL security and Brian O'Neil did it, but it wasn't a league-run deal, it was an information device for the clubs.

"These type of centers were becoming accepted in the '80s, and clubs had their own places which we wouldn't have heard about, so it wasn't all league-directed.

"The reason for . . . treatment is not to say you have a loophole. It is to say as a human being you can get help. Now, if we found out it was for illegal drugs, then you would lose your privilege to play.

"I talked to police, to confessed drug users . . . they said if you try to hide it, you will never be able to stop using it.

"Players would say, what about the NBA system . . . we had discussions, I remember Ron Francis saying to player reps [in 1990], 'I tell you, I don't want somebody on the ice carrying a stick who has been using that stuff.' That reflected the attitude of at least 75 to 80 percent of player reps. Back in the Murdoch era, it was 100 percent.

"When the NBA developed their program, I think the NBA did it and will tell you that they had such a bad problem in the league, they just couldn't suspend everyone. We were fortunate when Murdoch came along, we didn't have a bad problem, so we could say 'don't start.' We were fortunate we hadn't been infected like basketball or baseball.

"People forget we're a little private business, we're not the government, we're not General Motors. We set rules on how 'we' want to operate.

"Now, if someone comes to you and says I'm a coach and the reason I didn't come forward is because I didn't want a player to get suspended, then that coach better look at himself in the mirror. If [the player] didn't [get help] because he'd miss 30 games, if he thought it was more important he'd miss 30 games than get help, then they have a problem . . . but if you're asking me if I'd do it all again, then I'd say I wouldn't change a thing."

Following the Murdoch decision, Ziegler grafted three paragraphs from that text onto the text of every subsequent ruling he made. The paragraphs stressed the absolutism of the zero-tolerance principle, and the puritanical histrionics of player commitment to the game.

In 1989, though, a book written by Russian hockey star Igor Larionov confirmed that performance-enhancing drugs had arrived at the top levels of the game. In his book, *The Front Line Rebels,* Larionov claimed that Russian national team head coach Victor Tikhonov ordered players to take injections of an illegal substance. What was in the injections was not known to the players, Larionov said in the book, but they fooled drug testers at the 1986 world championships by submitting prepared urine vials that were planted behind toilet bowls for them. Larionov maintained that several players, including himself,

Viacheslav Fetisov, Sergei Makarov, Alexei Kasatonov, and Vladimir Krutov, refused to take the injections.

Larionov was immediately criticized by officials from the International Ice Hockey Federation. Larionov, then with the Vancouver Canucks, refused to comment further on his allegations. In Canada, though, Canadian Amateur Hockey Association (CAHA) head Murray Costello told the *Toronto Star* that the allegations announced a wake-up call for everyone in hockey who believed the game never had a problem with performance-enhancing drugs.

"With the type of schedules we have, a lot of games stretched over a long season, players need endurance more than anything and you wouldn't think there would be a drug problem," Costello said. "But at some of those championships, which are rather short-term, maybe they can peak for a week to ten days.

"It brings it to our attention; we can't ignore it. I'd be less than honest if I didn't say everyone in hockey is concerned, including the CAHA."

Many NHL players and coaches who traveled overseas to represent Canada in various international tournaments had long heard drug-related rumors circulating around the Russian national team. One NHL general manager said he was told that the injections were designed by Soviet doctors and integrated into the national team program on a regular basis. The general manager, who wished to remain unidentified, learned that to prepare the injections, the doctors would extract placenta from a pregnant woman and mix it with a honey-based liquid. The solution would then be injected directly into the digestive tracts of the players.

Kordic was also the subject of rumors circulating among players and coaches in the NHL. He made some incredible allegations to players he was close with, including one who is an active member of the NHLPA. The most famous allegation he made concerned a coach who happened into a hotel room where John and three or four other players were snorting cocaine. When the coach realized what he'd stumbled upon, he said hurriedly, "I didn't see that," then turned and left the room. John told over a dozen people about the incident. As the story was passed on, though, it became confused. John had said the incident took place in Toronto. He never specified whether it was a road game in Toronto while he was a member of the Canadiens, or if he was a Leaf at the time. It also became unclear whether the coach was indeed a head coach or an assistant. He simply said he would tell all in a book he was planning to write at the end of his career.

Other allegations John made included:

- How use of so-called recreational drugs—marijuana—and drinking were rampant on the junior hockey teams he'd played on;
- How some players, including a star Edmonton Oilers defenseman, took Echipoise to improve endurance and expedite healing of injuries;
- How cocaine "was a big thing on the Canadiens," even during the Stanley Cup year.
- How, as a Leaf, John met a player and NHLPA board member at Toronto's Pearson International Airport en route to rehab in Arizona. In a conversation, John said he had been "caught" using steroids, but that it was "all right" because he was receiving the drugs on prescription from the team. He also said he had a similar arrangement in Montreal with the Canadiens.

Virtually every coach John played for with the Leafs and Canadiens flatly rejected the allegation that steroids were provided for him through team prescriptions. They stressed the integrity of the medical profession, and underlined how tenuous and dangerous such an arrangement would be to the doctor involved. Common sense alone would dictate the allegation to be a fabrication, they argued. Players, coaches, and reporters knew John would create "truths" to convenience his own situation. A perfect case in point was his labeling Glen Sather a liar for failing to summon him from Cape Breton to Edmonton for the Stanley Cup play-offs. While John railed about broken promises and clauses in his contract, most who listened knew the opposite was true. They gave John the benefit of the doubt out of respect for his accomplishments; John wasn't hurting anyone, he was just being John. However, the player he spoke to at Pearson International Airport verified off the record that John indeed made that allegation.

"How do you think I felt?" the player said. "What if I have to go and fight one of these guys [enforcers] and they're on that stuff and I don't know about it . . ."

Five months after John died, the Quebec Major Junior Hockey League unveiled an alcohol- and drug-abuse policy for its players, the first of its kind in hockey. In part, the sensational aspects of John's death prompted league officials to develop the program.

In the fall of 1992, they distributed a comprehensive survey which asked if drug and alcohol problems exist in the league, and what possible responses could be taken towards prevention.

It was clear a drug policy was justifiable, based on the statistics compiled from the survey.

"We have a problem," league president Gilles Courteau said at the time. "It's minor, but we have to help the players, teach them what not to use. It's to their benefit. We have to take care of them, in hockey and in real life. Drugs and alcohol are part of real life."

The survey was delivered to 54 general managers, coaches, governors, therapists, and doctors from the league's 12 teams. Fifteen percent of the respondents said they believed the league's players were abusing drugs, alcohol, or steroids, while 34 percent said they believe there might be substance abuse among the players. Of the three substances—drugs, alcohol, and steroids—Courteau said he felt alcohol, notably beer, was the most frequently abused substance due to its price and availability. On the subject of alcohol, 64 percent of the respondents said there was no greater consumption of alcohol among the players than among the public. Another 31 percent said the consumption of alcohol among the players was lower than among the public.

In November 1994, the policy was completed and put into practice. The policy applied year-round, and targeted the prevention and detection of the use of "illegal substances, and to assist the players of the (league) who could have problems with drugs and alcohol." Here is a look at its contents:

POLICY ADMINISTRATION: Advisory Committee for the Assistance and Prevention Program (CAPAP) set up, with advisors available to consult players and team interveners on medical evaluations, treatments, and tests. Two doctors, one in Montreal and one in Quebec City, constitute the CAPAP.

TESTS FOR ILLEGAL ABUSE OF SUBSTANCES: All players subject to random testing during training camp, or at any other given time. Testing also done for "reasonable cause," which includes the following criteria: previous positive test, treatment, and/or arrest, and reasonable medical judgment of CAPAP or team doctor. Tests here can go on indefinitely and for the duration of the season. CAPAP can also "request a medical evaluation of each player who has been tested for reasonable cause, once a year." All testing follows protocol and procedures of the International Olympic Committee. Any player omission or refusal is considered equal to a positive test.

USE OF DRUGS: PROCEDURES FOLLOWING POSITIVE TESTING OR OTHER EVALUATION: Upon results of positive test, CAPAP advises player to treatment program. Player can request second test of sample B two days after first positive test, and can be present during analysis, and have present a qualified toxicologist, his lawyer, trainer, legal representative, or parents. Player evaluated through CAPAP, and disciplined if he refuses treatment program.

TO VOLUNTARILY ATTEND A TREATMENT PROGRAM: THE ADVANTAGE OF CONFIDENTIALITY: Upon voluntary disclosure by player, CAPAP will arrange evaluation and treatment, and will not inform team managers, doctors, or the league, unless player permits or has been hospitalized. No disciplinary measure for positive testing within 30 days following first voluntary disclosure to CAPAP.

ALCOHOLIC BEVERAGES: PROCEDURES FOLLOWING A CONVICTION RELATED TO THE CONSUMPTION OF ALCOHOL OR OTHER EVALUATION: Evaluation of player who breaks conduct rules contained in policy, with results forwarded to CAPAP, team doctor, and player. Team is responsible for ensuring that player attends evaluation center. Players receive written notice, evaluation, and CAPAP-recommended treatment upon first two occasions of breaking rules governing alcohol and drug abuse. A third infraction is referred to the league president, who collaborates with CAPAP to decide on a course of action.

THE RIGHT TO APPEAL: Player informed of positive test and/or disciplinary measure can appeal decision to the league president in writing five days following his notice. President renders decision in writing, and it is final.

At the same time the Quebec league program was put into effect, there was a changing of the guard in the NHL president's office. Stein's fatuous desire to be enshrined in the Hockey Hall of Fame came back to haunt him, and ultimately force his ousting in favor of Gary Bettman. Perhaps if Stein had used John's tragedy as the foundation for comprehensive change to the NHL stance on drugs, he may have improved the stability of his position. Instead, he became one of two immediate housecleaning chores Bettman inherited the minute he assumed office: investigations into Stein's hall-of-fame voting fraud, and the scandal in Ottawa in which it was alleged that the Senators purposely threw games to ensure themselves the first overall draft choice, which was undisputedly Alexandre Daigle.

From the beginning of his tenure, Bettman was denigrated because his career experience had nothing to do with hockey. A New Yorker, a lawyer, and a former high-ranking executive with the NBA, he became the subject of criticism and ridicule, especially in the Canadian press. None of it was more prevalent than during the labor dispute at the outset of the 1994–95 season which saw the owners enforce a lockout of the players. In Toronto, the press referred to him as a "New York lawyer"—in other words, an equation with the lowest of the low. His American roots surfaced among the daily controversies that fueled the animosity between the two sides in the lockout. It became like hockey's civil war, and among the players, he was cast as an imposing outsider, insensitive to Canadian players. Players took several opportunities to sling mud at him, none more celebrated than Chris Chelios's implied threats of harm coming to Bettman's family over the tension of the labor dispute. For several weeks afterward, he and his family lived alongside bodyguards. Wayne Gretzky, normally not one to publicly enter the fray, said Bettman was the owners' president, not the players'. The height of the bloodletting was reached in reports of other NHL front-office types fearing Bettman was being attacked on the grounds of anti-Semitic and anti-American prejudices among the Canadian players and press. Bettman responded to his detractors stoically. He said he believed Goodenow had ordered Gretzky, Chelios, and others to mount personal attacks, a ploy used by former baseball union boss Marvin Miller during acrimonious negotiations. In defense against the Gretzky charge, he told the *Chicago Tribune,* "Since I started here, we have signed a national TV deal with Fox, as well as major contracts with Nike and Anheuser-Busch. To me that can only benefit the players and the owners. I've been criticized heavily, primarily in Toronto, but the Oilers wouldn't still be in Edmonton today if it wasn't for me."

Bettman's hockey experience began with his first day on the job as NHL president. He grew up in Queens, New York, and pursued a career in law, graduating from Cornell University and the New York University of Law. He spent 12 years in the NBA as general counsel and senior vice president, a course that took him to third in the chain of command behind commissioner David Stern.

As the chief architect of the NBA's drug policy, Bettman brought a level of comprehension on the subject that was far superior to the middling knowledge of Stein and Ziegler. In fact, he knew more about drug policies and treatments than any of his predecessors in the history of the game.

Bettman readily stated he was prepared to open discussions with the players' union on a comprehensive drug policy. For the first time in the game's history, there was a willingness on both sides to bury the zero-tolerance policy in favor of a multistrike, aftercare treatment program. Goodenow and longtime NHL drug-policy critics like Patrick Ducharme were optimistic about Bettman's plan to bring about sensible change. However, for all the momentous promises from the game's preeminent power brokers, any real headway towards the league's first drug policy became a matter of when it could be introduced into CBA negotiations. A drug policy, despite its apparent urgency, was to be negotiated in the first renewal of the players' contract under Bettman. Both sides had been consulting experts with regards to preparing proposals. With the advent of the October 1994 lockout, though, the drug policy became a back-burner issue. The two sides became embroiled in the more immediate economic issues.

Bettman lent a positive indication of what could be under a new drug policy in his reaction to Bob Probert's sensational booze and drug run-in with police on July 15, 1994. Since there wasn't a new drug policy in place, Bettman found himself occupying the same position of bottom-line authority that Ziegler did in ruling over players with confirmed drug problems. While suspensions had always been guaranteed under Ziegler, Bettman chose to suspend Probert without pay and immediately placed him under the care Dr. Robert Lewis, a California-based specialist in substance-abuse treatment. The relevance of the term "suspension" was never clarified, mostly because Bettman refused to define the exact terms of his ruling. Probert was more accurately categorized as being on extended leave. He was treated by Dr. Lewis, then placed in a halfway house in Van Nuys. Each stop was a phase in his recovery, and Bettman carefully monitored the progress. Probert spent over four months in rehab, and was blessed with the birth of a daughter. Doctors treating him reported he had made significant progress towards a full recovery. Bettman, though, declined to announce a return date, even though Probert appeared ready to rejoin hockey by February 1995.

Within Bettman's holding pattern, Probert's future as a player was effectively weighed against his future survival. In a nine-day span following his run-in with police, he was released by the Detroit Red Wings and picked up by the Chicago Blackhawks on a four-year, $6.6 million contract. The longer Probert remained in rehab, the greater the likelihood of losing a year's salary of the richest contract he ever signed. Moreover, there was no clear indication whether Bettman would attach a multigame sentence to his suspension, which would presumably be without pay, as well.

The question mark surrounding Probert stemmed from a July 15 incident in which he crashed his motorcycle into a car while driving in West Bloomfield, Michigan. His blood-alcohol level was found to be 0.31, more than three times the legal limit. He spent a night in hospital, and after being charged with drunk driving, was released on a $10,000 bond. Court records later showed that police had obtained a warrant permitting them to take samples of his blood while he was in the emergency ward following his accident. The samples were sent to the Michigan State police lab in Lansing, along with a form specifying "cocaine suspected, please test for both cocaine and alcohol." When the lab results were returned in early August, it showed Probert to have "a presumptive presence of cocaine in his blood." The report also suggested that he ingested the cocaine two hours or less before being hospitalized following the accident. Albert Holtz, Probert's attorney, challenged the legality of the police search warrant in court. He contended that the police ordered a test for cocaine only after improperly viewing confidential medical reports. The legality of the warrant was later upheld in a January 1995 court ruling.

Beyond the alarming details of the revelations in the press, Probert gave every indication he was mired in the same hell that descended on John. From police accounts of the scene, Probert's behavior was strangely volatile and sad. He cursed and threatened police and hospital workers with death, then broke into tears and had to be restrained. The overall picture of that night suggests that Probert didn't just have a drug- and alcohol-related accident, he had a close brush with death.

"In short strokes, what I saw was somebody [Probert] who agreed he had a chronic problem," Bettman said in a February 1995 interview. "I wanted to break the cycle because I didn't see the player having too many more opportunities . . . This was a player who could end up killing himself.

"Whether he plays hockey again is not my concern. Whether he leads a sober life is a priority. I'm not ready to focus on when he's ready. Let them [rehab experts] determine when he is ready to get out of treatment, then take it from there. If he never plays again . . . I think it's too premature to discuss that, but having said that, I don't think I can begin to discuss that until the course of his recovery is evaluated. If he has a sober life, I will be satisfied that the steps we took were the right ones."

Bettman continued to educate himself on substance abuse and treatments throughout the 1994–95 season. There was a particular uniqueness to the definition of the problems existing in the NHL. As architect of the NBA drug policy, Bettman quickly realized the focus of that policy—cocaine—did not readily apply to the experience of the NHL. In professional hockey, alcohol abuse historically registered as the preeminent problem among players. There had been a litany of alcohol-related incidents—deaths of some of the game's brightest stars and dozens of infamous drunk driving charges, barroom brawls, and even alleged sexual assaults—that had, in a disturbing fashion, never been effectively dealt with by the league. Players were traditionally advised against all substance abuse, gambling, prostitution, and a host of other social maladies, by the NHL's security staff. That advice was levied during training camps. Afterward, the player had the option of phoning a security agent if a problem arose. As with drug abuse, individual teams were left to further educate players on alcohol abuse. The NHLPA also proffered counselors for the same purpose. Approximately 12 NHL teams offer free cab rides to players who overindulge, no questions asked. However, in terms of one identifiable policy which would offer a definitive education and treatment program, the NHL has sadly neglected its responsibilities, and has consequently left many skeletons in the closet. Some of them came out during the early phases of Bettman's tenure.

In March 1994, five months before Probert's dangerous binge, alarm bells went off in Hartford with the Whalers' players and management. Six players—captain Pat Verbeek, Todd Harkins, Marc Potvin, Mark Janssens,

Chris Pronger, Geoff Sanderson, and assistant coach Kevin McCarthy—were arrested after an incident at a Buffalo nightclub. Five days later, Pronger was arrested on drunk-driving charges, while Bryan Marchment was arrested on similar charges two weeks later. When the players posed for their team picture in mid-April, general manager Paul Holmgren was conspicuous by his absence. At the time, he was an in-patient at the Betty Ford Center in California for alcohol abuse treatment following a drunk-driving arrest on March 31. Ten alcohol-related arrests in less than a month, a stat as significant as the team's dismal 27–48–9 record.

In subsequent reports on the apparent problem, team owners, coaches, and the players themselves insisted that the level of drinking on the team was no more, or no less, than any of the other 25 teams in the NHL. According to other newspaper reports, the 1988–89 Detroit Red Wings had six recovering alcoholics on their roster, while Pierre Page said that on all three teams he served with—Calgary, Minnesota, and Quebec—there were players receiving treatment for drug and/or alcohol abuse. One Leaf general manager said Miroslav Frycer had twice been arrested on drunk-driving charges, and Bill Derlago was well known to police for handing out game tickets when he was pulled over in obvious drinking-and-driving situations. Meanwhile, just after Christmas 1993, Pittsburgh Penguins' general manager Craig Patrick was in a single car crash which resulted in a drunk-driving charge. Just after the Whalers' incident in Buffalo, Penguins' Tom Barrasso, Peter Taglianetti, and strength coach John Welday were arrested after a fight in a bar. On February 6, 1994, Chicago Blackhawks owner William Wirtz pleaded guilty to driving under the influence of alcohol three months earlier. On a more positive note, Bryan Fogarty had earned a job with the Montreal Canadiens and Louis DeBrusk with Edmonton, both appearing to have successfully recovered from alcoholism.

More than in any other sport, hockey's marketing success, from the early stages of minor right up to the pro level, has in large part been linked with breweries. The vast majority of today's players would not have played in

Memorial Cups, or won awards, had it not been for brewery sponsorships. Part of that landscape, though, is the accessibility to beer products, through arena lounges, for example, where drinking becomes a socially acceptable extension of the game experience, for both fans and players. It comes as no surprise, then, that one of the most commonly told stories regarding Fogarty centers on his introduction to drinking early on in his playing career. As a 14-year-old, his ability vaulted him into competition with 16-, 17-, and 18-year-olds. It was commonplace to drink regularly after games, and Fogarty followed in the footsteps of his peers.

Links between beer and hockey date back as far as the 1930s when Wirtz's father, Arthur M. Wirtz, was rising to power among NHL owners. The elder Wirtz, together with James Norris, a real estate speculator at the time who would go on to have an NHL division named after him (Norris Division), purchased two of the great arenas in the game, in Chicago and Detroit. Wirtz was also a major liquor distributor and popularized hockey among fans, in part by selling his product at games.

In the 1993–94 season, seven NHL media guides featured full-page beer ads on the back cover, while five teams were, or had been, financed largely by the alcohol-related industry: Wirtz in Chicago; Molson Breweries owning the Canadiens since 1978, and 20 percent of the Leafs between 1990 and 1994; Anheuser-Busch owning a portion of the St. Louis Blues; Carling O'Keefe as majority owners of the Nordiques between 1976 and 1988.

Following the Whalers' incidents, and the knowledge he gained from his own research, Bettman began telling reporters that education against alcohol abuse would bear the principle focus in a new league substance-abuse policy. He could see elements of the NBA policy he helped create being carried over into the NHL. The major difference, though, was considerations based on the two substances—alcohol being legal, and cocaine illegal. Part of the education would likely have to provide conduct guidelines for responsible drinking, drinking and driving, underage drinking, and drinking in bars.

"I was one of the architects of it [NBA policy], but that

doesn't mean you take it over here [the NHL] on a cookie-cutter basis," Bettman said. "I think the NBA program focuses more on illegal drugs like cocaine. I think it would be more appropriate for us to look at it from an education standpoint, against alcohol. You tailor your [policy] to your player population."

Bettman gave the press limited insights into an eventual NHL drug policy; he knew how to answer questions with a politician's graceful diplomacy. One of the first communiqués he issued was a gag order to NHL owners, emphasizing the importance of airing their beefs in private and not in the press. It was unfortunate for his sake that the press, in the heat of the lockout, directed its capacity for satire at him, and rarely acknowledged his élan. He indicated that the NHL and the players' association were on the same page with regards to several elements in a drug policy, including: multi-strikes for admitted substance abusers; counselors approved by the league and NHLPA; and after-care treatment and education. He also conceded—marginally—the players' longtime stance against drug testing, which Goodenow stressed would not change in negotiations for a new drug policy.

"I view this [the elements that will comprise a new drug policy] as problem solving, not negotiating," Bettman said. "This is something we need to reason on, and come up with something compatible. My personal feelings on testing are not relevant. I'm not coming into this with a predisposition, I'm coming with a desire to make sure it's effective. The issue is not testing, but why are you testing. To test is not something you do for the sake of doing it. People would debate whether it's smart to test for punishment or for educating a player. You can't do testing in a vacuum, it has to be done in a comprehensive drug plan. I think people look for simple answers. It's what will work, what the players will accept."

For all the promise of his rhetoric, Bettman declined comment on John Kordic's situation. He claimed the NHL's dealings with John were part of another leadership regime. The NHL, though, its owners, general managers, coaches, and players, treaded on dangerous ground in their attempts to keep John's problems under wraps. Though he'd

passed on, John's tragedy provided a lesson of the hypoc-
risy of how drinking and drugs were dealt with under the
NHL's then-prevailing attitudes towards substance abuse.
John tenaciously held on denying his drug use. Ducharme
likened the condition to the hallmark of an addict, while
Dr. Fearing, who was privy to John's demons, said he had
a "terminal uniqueness," a belief that everything bad associated with drug use wouldn't happen to him because he
was different, a hockey player. John, though, knew that if
he admitted to alcohol abuse, the worst-case scenario was
rehab. There was plenty of evidence to back that up since
the league had suspended five players for drug abuse, but
in the numerous alcohol-related offenses, the NHL never
once suspended a player. In that respect, he had a ready
excuse to help him live a lie. That lie became an absurdity
when John was rehabbed for alcohol abuse.

There were two schools of thought on John's apparent
alcohol dependency: one was carried by Bryan Fogarty,
who said they shared the same daily battles in fighting the
disease; the other was postulated by Bruce Cashman, who
said John was not an alcoholic; rather, he drank in accom-
paniment to his cocaine habit. If the conclusions of the
inquest into John's death have any weight, the overriding
indication is that John's premiere dependency was on cocaine, not alcohol. The question, then, is why, after everything the doctors, coaches, and general managers saw, was
John assigned to alcohol rehab? To be sure, John's dependency on cocaine was far more complex than his coaches,
or the league, were prepared to deal with. It was a problem—compounded by steroid use—that was never re-
motely understood. All those who handled him professed
to going above and beyond the call of duty to help. John's
problems, though, were not a "project" for Pierre Page or
Doug Carpenter to take on, with some grand illusion of
succeeding where all others failed. Nor do those efforts, as
ingenuous as they were, somehow absolve hockey from
the tragedy of John's demise. Rather, among the many
arguments about his passing, there is one certain truth:
John was neither an alcoholic nor a drug addict until he
started playing professional hockey. That alone should

stand as a warning to those players and officials with the responsibility of developing a new substance-abuse policy: do your homework with each individual case—it will be the only hope of preventing another tragedy like John's from happening.

Here is a look at what shape a new NHL drug policy might take, based on a draft proposal submitted to the league by Patrick Ducharme. The proposal is a response to materials the league had previously considered as fundamental to a new policy:

EDUCATION: Careful selection of educators who understand an athlete's unique character and lifestyle. Athletes usually feel under abnormal pressure to succeed. They also tend to mistakenly think of themselves as special, impervious, and are often prey to long, unfilled hours in which the lure of drugs and alcohol becomes overwhelming. Educators should then be knowledgeable about addictions, communicate easily with athletes, and not be fazed by people of celebrity status. Program should be given to problem as well as nonproblem players, for the benefit of all.

ACCESS-CONFIDENTIALITY: Players "must be assured that their contact with specially trained counselor(s) will not be known to the league or to the team without player's consent." Without this assurance, a player, and people, in general, tend "to deny the existence of addictive behaviour rather than admitting it. The denial is often not a conscious choice." If a player "never knows from one day to the next whether he will still be playing for the team he was on yesterday, the fear of punishment, trade, demotion, or loss of job complicates the already serious problem of the insidious disease of alcoholism or drug abuse."

AFTER-CARE: Withdrawal, and elimination, of drug testing following drug-abuse treatment, as suggested in other documents presented to the NHL. Mandatory drug testing stigmatizes the problem, fosters denial, and smacks of punishment. Experience of after-care workers will ensure patients are following the treatment program. After-care is not a cure; there is no cure for addictive behavior.

Hence, after-care should be understood as a lifelong project and continued treatment. Also, discontinued requirement of treated players to attend group therapy sessions with Alcoholics Anonymous and Narcotics Anonymous, and so on, based on the athlete's celebrity status impeding treatment in large groups. "I remember one counselor describing to me the difficulty in treating Bob Probert . . . on how difficult it was to convince Bob that there was a continuing problem when all the rest of the members in the group continually asked for his autograph and sought his favor so that they could 'hang around' with him or get tickets from him." Ideal administration is intensive individual therapy done privately and confidentially, followed with an option of group treatment, "so long as the group consists of only professional athletes."

ALCOHOL-ABUSE TREATMENT: Continuation of player's pay, and no penalty of any kind while under treatment for alcohol abuse. Relapses should be expected, and counselors reveal how they can be used "as tools to effect behavioral change . . ." Financial penalty "overlooks the true nature of the disease. Generally, the person in treatment does not want to relapse. Often, the disease has been present in the player for many years . . . financial penalty connected with [relapse] will adversely affect the relationship between counselor and player and inhibit honesty. Addictive behavior is often based on fear—fear of failure, rejection . . . Good counselors use that same fear to effect treatment . . . As one counselor said to his patient: 'You may have one more drunk left in you but I fear that you do not have one more recovery' . . . The player has to replace his other fears with the fear of relapse."

THREE-STRIKE APPROACH: "A player who violates his first strike after [treatment] and who comes forward for additional treatment should be allowed that treatment while continuing to be paid and with no penalty of any kind imposed so long as the player follows and adheres to the treatment." Also, withdrawal of suspension at half-pay for the duration of second-strike treatment. According to statistics from the Brentwood Recovery Home in Windsor, approximately 50 percent of persons recover on first treatment, while 25 percent achieve recovery on second treatment. Thus, no penalty of any kind imposed on first- and second-strike player. On third strike, alter the suspension from "permanent" to "indefinite." A third-strike player should also have the right to appeal the suspension, through an independent arbiter. "By including the NHL president and the program director as panellists, you invite political wrangling between persons with their own special interests . . . All the rules of natural justice should apply in the appeal . . . that is, the player should have the right to be independently represented by counsel of his choice; he should be given full disclosure of the allegations made against him; and he should be afforded adequate opportunity to prepare and present a full answer and defence . . ."

REQUIRED TREATMENT: Withdrawal of the necessity of a player arrested for a serious drug offense to enter the league's treatment program with two strikes. Instead, upon arrest, the program should be "offered to" the player, but not become mandatory until conviction or entry of a guilty plea. If a player is convicted of a serious drug offense (trafficking), he will likely receive a jail term, and the league will be justified in levying its own punishment. If a player is convicted of a minor offense (possession), the court punishment is usually a fine and/or probation, and there is no need for the league to intervene with its own punishment . . . "the league's focus should remain on treatment."

PROHIBITED SUBSTANCES: The Narcotic Control Act of Canada and the Food and Drug Act of Canada can be used to define a list of prohibited substances under the NHL policy.

PROGRAM ADMINISTRATION, QUALITY ASSURANCE: Player/counselor relationship to be reviewed under an agreed-upon mechanism. "Again, I lean on Bob Probert's experience in this area. Bob Probert was subjected to a large number of treatment counselors. Many of them were ineffective and their lack of effectiveness was not related simply to the lack of effort on their parts or to Bob's own attitude or effect. Feeling obligated to comply with the team's request for treatment, Bob labored through innumerable shopping trips with one counselor who could think of no other way to interact with him than to accompany Bob on these trips. Bob always went along, feeling that he was pleasing the counselor but privately deploring the requirement. A change from that counselor to another produced remarkable changes in the effectiveness of treatment. If a player has the ability to outline reasonable grounds for requesting a different counselor after 30 days, more effective treatment is likely to result." In addition, the team must be excluded from involvement in when or how the treatment progresses. "Probert's treatment was occasionally interrupted and . . . undermined because the team [Detroit] insisted that he continue practice."

Index